PENGUIN BOOKS — GREAT IDEAS
On the Nature of War

1. Seneca *On the Shortness of Life*
2. Marcus Aurelius *Meditations*
3. St Augustine *Confessions of a Sinner*
4. Thomas à Kempis *The Inner Life*
5. Niccolò Machiavelli *The Prince*
6. Michel de Montaigne *On Friendship*
7. Jonathan Swift *A Tale of a Tub*
8. Jean-Jacques Rousseau *The Social Contract*
9. Edward Gibbon *The Christians and the Fall of Rome*
10. Thomas Paine *Common Sense*
11. Mary Wollstonecraft *A Vindication of the Rights of Woman*
12. William Hazlitt *On the Pleasure of Hating*
13. Karl Marx & Friedrich Engels *The Communist Manifesto*
14. Arthur Schopenhauer *On the Suffering of the World*
15. John Ruskin *On Art and Life*
16. Charles Darwin *On Natural Selection*
17. Friedrich Nietzsche *Why I am So Wise*
18. Virginia Woolf *A Room of One's Own*
19. Sigmund Freud *Civilization and Its Discontents*
20. George Orwell *Why I Write*

21. Confucius *The First Ten Books*
22. Sun-tzu *The Art of War*
23. Plato *The Symposium*
24. Lucretius *Sensation and Sex*
25. Cicero *An Attack on an Enemy of Freedom*
26. *The Revelation of St John the Divine* and *The Book of Job*
27. Marco Polo *Travels in the Land of Kubilai Khan*
28. Christine de Pizan *The City of Ladies*
29. Baldesar Castiglione *How to Achieve True Greatness*
30. Francis Bacon *Of Empire*
31. Thomas Hobbes *Of Man*
32. Sir Thomas Browne *Urne-Burial*
33. Voltaire *Miracles and Idolatry*
34. David Hume *On Suicide*
35. Carl von Clausewitz *On the Nature of War*
36. Søren Kierkegaard *Fear and Trembling*
37. Henry David Thoreau *Where I Lived, and What I Lived For*
38. Thorstein Veblen *Conspicuous Consumption*
39. Albert Camus *The Myth of Sisyphus*
40. Hannah Arendt *Eichmann and the Holocaust*

Carl von Clausewitz
1780–1831

Carl von Clausewitz

On the Nature of War

TRANSLATED BY
J. GRAHAM

PENGUIN BOOKS — GREAT IDEAS

PENGUIN BOOKS

Published by the Penguin Group
Penguin Books Ltd, 80 Strand, London WC2R 0RL, England
Penguin Group (USA) Inc., 375 Hudson Street, New York, New York 10014, USA
Penguin Group (Canada), 10 Alcorn Avenue, Toronto, Ontario, Canada M4V 3B2
(a division of Pearson Penguin Canada Inc.)
Penguin Ireland, 25 St Stephen's Green, Dublin 2, Ireland
(a division of Penguin Books Ltd)
Penguin Group (Australia), 250 Camberwell Road,
Camberwell, Victoria 3124, Australia (a division of Pearson Australia Group Pty Ltd)
Penguin Books India Pvt Ltd, 11 Community Centre,
Panchsheel Park, New Delhi – 110 017, India
Penguin Group (NZ), cnr Airborne and Rosedale Roads, Albany,
Auckland 1310, New Zealand (a division of Pearson New Zealand Ltd)
Penguin Books (South Africa) (Pty) Ltd, 24 Sturdee Avenue,
Rosebank 2196, South Africa

Penguin Books Ltd, Registered Offices: 80 Strand, London WC2R 0RL, England

www.penguin.com

Vom Kriege first published 1832
This translation first published by Routledge & Kegan Paul 1908
Published in Penguin Classics 1982
This extract published in Penguin Books 2005

1

Taken from the Penguin Classics edition of
On War, edited by Anatol Rapoport

Set by Rowland Phototypesetting Ltd, Bury St Edmunds, Suffolk
Printed in England by Clays Ltd, St Ives plc

Except in the United States of America, this book is sold subject
to the condition that it shall not, by way of trade or otherwise, be lent,
re-sold, hired out, or otherwise circulated without the publisher's
prior consent in any form of binding or cover other than that in
which it is published and without a similar condition including this
condition being imposed on the subsequent purchaser

Contents

Introduction of the Author   1

What is War?   5
End and Means in War   36
Branches of the Art of War   38
On the Theory of War   51
Art or Science of War   82
Methodicism   86
Criticism   95
On Examples   100

Introduction of the Author

That the conception of the scientific does not consist alone, or chiefly, in system, and its finished theoretical constructions, requires nowadays no exposition. System in this treatise is not to be found on the surface, and instead of a finished building of theory, there are only materials.

The scientific form lies here in the endeavour to explore the nature of military phenomena to show their affinity with the nature of the things of which they are composed. Nowhere has the philosophical argument been evaded, but where it runs out into too thin a thread the Author has preferred to cut it short, and fall back upon the corresponding results of experience; for in the same way as many plants only bear fruit when they do not shoot too high, so in the practical arts the theoretical leaves and flowers must not be made to sprout too far, but kept near to experience, which is their proper soil.

Unquestionably it would be a mistake to try to discover from the chemical ingredients of a grain of corn the form of the ear of corn which it bears, as we have only to go to the field to see the ears ripe. Investigation and observation, philosophy and experience, must neither despise nor exclude one another; they mutually afford each other the rights of citizenship. Consequently, the propositions of this book, with their arch of inherent necessity, are supported either by experience or by the conception of War itself as external points, so that they are not without abutments.

It is, perhaps, not impossible to write a systematic theory of War full of spirit and substance, but ours, hitherto, have been very much the reverse. To say nothing of their unscientific spirit, in their striving after coherence and completeness of system, they overflow with commonplaces, truisms, and twaddle of every kind. If we want a striking picture of them we have only to read Lichtenberg's extract from a code of regulations in case of fire.

If a house takes fire, we must seek, above all things, to protect the right side of the house standing on the left, and, on the other hand, the left side of the house on the right; for if we, for example should protect the left side of the house on the left, then the right side of the house lies to the right of the left, and consequently as the fire lies to the right of this side, and of the right side (for we have assumed that the house is situated to the left of the fire), therefore the right side is situated nearer to the fire than the left, and the right side of the house might catch fire if it was not protected before it came to the left, which is protected. Consequently, something might be burnt that is not protected, and that sooner than something else would be burnt, even if it was not protected; consequently we must let alone the latter and protect the former. In order to impress the thing on one's mind, we have only to note if the house is situated to the right of the fire, then it is the left side, and if the house is to the left it is the right side.

On the Nature of War

In order not to frighten the intelligent reader by such commonplaces, and to make the little good that there is distasteful by pouring water upon it, the Author has preferred to give in small ingots of fine metal his impressions and convictions, the result of many years' reflection on War, of his intercourse with men of ability, and of much personal experience. Thus the seemingly weakly bound-together chapters of this book have arisen, but it is hoped they will not be found wanting in logical connexion. Perhaps soon a greater head may appear, and instead of these single grains, give the whole in a casting of pure metal without dross.

In order to fignite the intelligence already our own impress, and to miss the truth, and that the air dangerous to policy-makers, if not the author, the potential to develop it at any cost of the press the tropics, sions and distraction. The reason is many ways a different burden, of almost out of the equipment of which, in the moment prudent experiment. Stan the example, easily formed together pleasure or one who lives in the com-munity, he will no not be bound wanting in logical contest anyway creature means, and may appear, and in not, or, it is a much point, give the whole in a variety or panacea, but without draws.

What is War?

1. Introduction

We propose to consider first the single elements of our subject, then each branch or part, and, last of all, the whole, in all its relations – therefore to advance from the simple to the complex. But it is necessary for us to commence with a glance at the nature of the whole, because it is particularly necessary that in the consideration of any of the parts their relation to the whole should be kept constantly in view.

2. Definition

We shall not enter into any of the abstruse definitions of War used by publicists. We shall keep to the element of the thing itself, to a duel. War is nothing but a duel on an extensive scale. If we would conceive as a unit the countless number of duels which make up a War, we shall do so best by supposing to ourselves two wrestlers. Each strives by physical force to compel the other to submit to his will: each endeavours to throw his adversary, and thus render him incapable of further resistance.

War therefore is an act of violence intended to compel our opponent to fulfil our will.

Violence arms itself with the inventions of Art and Science in order to contend against violence. Self-imposed restrictions, almost imperceptible and hardly worth mentioning, termed usages of International Law, accompany it without essentially impairing its power. Violence, that is to say, physical force (for there is no moral force without the conception of States and Law), is therefore the *means*; the compulsory submission of the enemy to our will is the ultimate *object*. In order to attain this object fully, the enemy must be disarmed, and disarmament becomes therefore the immediate object of hostilities in theory. It takes the place of the final object, and puts it aside as something we can eliminate from our calculations.

3. Utmost use of force

Now, philanthropists may easily imagine there is a skilful method of disarming and overcoming an enemy without causing great bloodshed, and that this is the proper tendency of the Art of War. However plausible this may appear, still it is an error which must be extirpated; for in such dangerous things as War, the errors which proceed from a spirit of benevolence are the worst. As the use of physical power to the utmost extent by no means excludes the cooperation of the intelligence, it follows that he who uses force unsparingly, without reference to the bloodshed involved, must obtain a superiority if his adversary uses less vigour in its application. The former then dictates the law to the latter, and both proceed to extremities to which the only limitations are those imposed by the amount of counteracting force on each side.

This is the way in which the matter must be viewed, and it is to no purpose, it is even against one's own interest, to turn away from the consideration of the real nature of the affair because the horror of its elements excites repugnance.

If the Wars of civilized people are less cruel and destructive than those of savages, the difference arises from the social condition both of States in themselves and in their relations to each other. Out of this social condition and its relations War arises, and by it War is subjected to conditions, is controlled and modified. But these things do not belong to War itself; they are only given conditions; and to introduce into the philosophy of War itself a principle of moderation would be an absurdity.

Two motives lead men to War: instinctive hostility and hostile intention. In our definition of War, we have chosen as its characteristic the latter of these elements, because it is the most general. It is impossible to conceive the passion of hatred of the wildest description, bordering on mere instinct, without combining with it the idea of a hostile intention. On the other hand, hostile intentions may often exist without being accompanied by any, or at all events by any extreme, hostility of feeling. Amongst savages views emanating from the feelings, amongst civilized nations those emanating from the understanding, have the predominance; but this difference arises from attendant circumstances, existing institutions, etc., and, therefore, is not to be found necessarily in all cases, although it prevails in the majority. In short, even the most civilized nations may burn with passionate hatred of each other.

We may see from this what a fallacy it would be to refer the War of a civilized nation entirely to an intelligent act on the part of the Government, and to imagine it as continually freeing itself more and more from all feeling of passion in such a way that at last the physical masses of combatants would no longer be required; in reality, their mere relations would suffice – a kind of algebraic action.

Theory was beginning to drift in this direction until the facts of the last War taught it better. If War is an *act* of force, it belongs necessarily also to the feelings. If it does not originate in the feelings, it *reacts*, more or less, upon them, and the extent of this reaction depends not on the degree of civilization, but upon the importance and duration of the interests involved.

Therefore, if we find civilized nations do not put their prisoners to death, do not devastate towns and countries, this is because their intelligence exercises greater influence on their mode of carrying on War, and has taught them more effectual means of applying force than these rude acts of mere instinct. The invention of gunpowder, the constant progress of improvements in the construction of firearms, are sufficient proofs that the tendency to destroy the adversary which lies at the bottom of the conception of War is in no way changed or modified through the progress of civilization.

We therefore repeat our proposition, that War is an

act of violence pushed to its utmost bounds; as one side dictates the law to the other, there arises a sort of reciprocal action, which logically must lead to an extreme. This is the first reciprocal action, and the first extreme with which we meet (*first reciprocal action*).

4. *The aim is to disarm the enemy*

We have already said that the aim of all action in War is to disarm the enemy, and we shall now show that this, theoretically at least, is indispensable.

If our opponent is to be made to comply with our will, we must place him in a situation which is more oppressive to him than the sacrifice which we demand; but the disadvantages of this position must naturally not be of a transitory nature, at least in appearance, otherwise the enemy, instead of yielding, will hold out, in the prospect of a change for the better. Every change in this position which is produced by a continuation of the War should therefore be a change for the worse. The worst condition in which a belligerent can be placed is that of being completely disarmed. If, therefore, the enemy is to be reduced to submission by an act of War, he must either be positively disarmed or placed in such a position that he is threatened with it. From this it follows that the disarming or overthrow of the enemy, whichever we call it, must always be the aim of Warfare. Now War is always the shock of two hostile bodies in collision, not the action of a living power upon an inanimate mass, because an absolute state of endurance would not be making War; therefore, what we have just said as to the aim of action in War applies to both parties. Here, then, is another case of reciprocal action. As long as the enemy is not defeated, he may defeat me; then I shall be no longer my own master; he will dictate the law to me as I did to him. This is the second reciprocal action, and leads to a second extreme (*second reciprocal action*).

5. *Utmost exertion of powers*

If we desire to defeat the enemy, we must proportion our efforts to his powers of resistance. This is expressed by the product of two factors which cannot be separated, namely, *the sum of available means* and *the strength of the Will*. The sum of the available means may be estimated in a measure, as it depends (although not entirely) upon numbers; but the strength of volition is more difficult to determine, and can only be estimated to a certain extent by the strength of the motives. Granted we have obtained in this way an approximation to the strength of the power to be contended with, we can then take a review of our own means, and either increase them so as to obtain a preponderance, or, in case we have not the resources to effect this, then do our best by increasing our means as far as possible. But the adversary does the same; therefore, there is a new mutual enhancement, which, in pure conception, must create a fresh effort towards an extreme. This is the third case of reciprocal action, and a third extreme with which we meet (*third reciprocal action*).

6. Modification in the reality

Thus reasoning in the abstract, the mind cannot stop short of an extreme, because it has to deal with an extreme, with a conflict of forces left to themselves, and obeying no other but their own inner laws. If we should seek to deduce from the pure conception of War an absolute point for the aim which we shall propose and for the means which we shall apply, this constant reciprocal action would involve us in extremes, which would be nothing but a play of ideas produced by an almost invisible train of logical subtleties. If, adhering closely to the absolute, we try to avoid all difficulties by a stroke of the pen, and insist with logical strictness that in every case the extreme must be the object, and the utmost effort must be exerted in that direction, such a stroke of the pen would be a mere paper law, not by any means adapted to the real world.

Even supposing this extreme tension of forces was an absolute which could easily be ascertained, still we must admit that the human mind would hardly submit itself to this kind of logical chimera. There would be in many cases an unnecessary waste of power, which would be in opposition to other principles of statecraft; an effort of Will would be required disproportioned to the proposed object, which therefore it would be impossible to realize, for the human will does not derive its impulse from logical subtleties.

But everything takes a different shape when we pass from abstractions to reality. In the former, everything must be subject to optimism, and we must imagine the one side as well as the other striving after perfection and even attaining it. Will this ever take place in reality? It will if,

(1). War becomes a completely isolated act, which arises suddenly, and is in no way connected with the previous history of the combatant States.
(2). If it is limited to a single solution, or to several simultaneous solutions.
(3). If it contains within itself the solution perfect and complete, free from any reaction upon it, through a calculation beforehand of the political situation which will follow from it.

7. *War is never an isolated act*

With regard to the first point, neither of the two opponents is an abstract person to the other, not even as regards that factor in the sum of resistance which does not depend on objective things, viz. the Will. This Will is not an entirely unknown quantity; it indicates what it will be tomorrow by what it is today. War does not spring up quite suddenly, it does not spread to the full in a moment; each of the two opponents can, therefore, form an opinion of the other, in a great measure, from what he is and what he does, instead of judging of him according to what he, strictly speaking, should be or should do. But, now, man with his incomplete organization is always below the line of absolute perfection, and thus these deficiencies, having an influence on both sides, become a modifying principle.

8. War does not consist of a single instantaneous blow

The second point gives rise to the following considerations:

If War ended in a single solution, or a number of simultaneous ones, then naturally all the preparations for the same would have a tendency to the extreme, for an omission could not in any way be repaired; the utmost, then, that the world of reality could furnish as a guide for us would be the preparations of the enemy, as far as they are known to us; all the rest would fall into the domain of the abstract. But if the result is made up from several successive acts, then naturally that which precedes with all its phases may be taken as a measure for that which will follow, and in this manner the world of reality again takes the place of the abstract, and thus modifies the effort towards the extreme.

Yet every War would necessarily resolve itself into a single solution, or a sum of simultaneous results, if all the means required for the struggle were raised at once, or could be at once raised; for as one adverse result necessarily diminishes the means, then if all the means have been applied in the first, a second cannot properly be supposed. All hostile acts which might follow would belong essentially to the first, and form in reality only its duration.

But we have already seen that even in the preparation for War the real world steps into the place of mere abstract conception – a material standard into the place of the hypotheses of an extreme: that therefore in that way both parties, by the influence of the mutual reaction, remain below the line of extreme effort, and therefore all forces are not at once brought forward.

It lies also in the nature of these forces and their application that they cannot all be brought into activity at the same time. These forces are *the armies actually on foot, the country,* with its superficial extent and its population, *and the allies.*

In point of fact, the country, with its superficial area and the population, besides being the source of all military force, constitutes in itself an integral part of the efficient quantities in War, providing either the theatre of war or exercising a considerable influence on the same.

Now, it is possible to bring all the movable military forces of a country into operation at once, but not all fortresses, rivers, mountains, people, etc. – in short, not the whole country, unless it is so small that it may be completely embraced by the first act of the War. Further, the cooperation of allies does not depend on the Will of the belligerents; and from the nature of the political relations of states to each other, this cooperation is frequently not afforded until after the War has commenced, or it may be increased to restore the balance of power.

That this part of the means of resistance, which cannot at once be brought into activity, in many cases, is a much greater part of the whole than might at first be supposed, and that it often restores the balance of power, seriously affected by the great force of the first decision, will be more fully shown hereafter. Here it is sufficient to show that a complete concentration of all available means in a moment of time is contradictory to the nature of War.

Now this, in itself, furnishes no ground for relaxing our efforts to accumulate strength to gain the first result, because an unfavourable issue is always a disadvantage to which no one would purposely expose himself, and also because the first decision, although not the only one, still will have the more influence on subsequent events, the greater it is in itself.

But the possibility of gaining a later result causes men to take refuge in that expectation, owing to the repugnance in the human mind to making excessive efforts; and therefore forces are not concentrated and measures are not taken for the first decision with that energy which would otherwise be used. Whatever one belligerent omits from weakness, becomes to the other a real objective ground for limiting his own efforts, and thus again, through this reciprocal action, extreme tendencies are brought down to efforts on a limited scale.

9. *The result in war is never absolute*

Lastly, even the final decision of a whole War is not always to be regarded as absolute. The conquered State often sees in it only a passing evil, which may be repaired in after times by means of political combinations. How much this must modify the degree of tension, and the vigour of the efforts made, is evident in itself.

10. *The probabilities of real life take the place of the conceptions of the extreme and the absolute*

In this manner, the whole act of War is removed from the rigorous law of forces exerted to the utmost. If the extreme is no longer to be apprehended, and no longer to be sought for, it is left to the judgement to determine the limits for the efforts to be made in place of it, and this can only be done on the data furnished by the facts of the real world by the *laws of probability*. Once the belligerents are no longer mere conceptions, but individual States and Governments, once the War is no longer an ideal, but a definite substantial procedure, then the reality will furnish the data to compute the unknown quantities which are required to be found.

From the character, the measures, the situation of the adversary, and the relations with which he is surrounded, each side will draw conclusions by the law of probability as to the designs of the other, and act accordingly.

11. *The political object now reappears*

Here the question which we had laid aside forces itself again into consideration, *viz. the political object of the War*. The law of the extreme, the view to disarm the adversary, to overthrow him, has hitherto to a certain extent usurped the place of this end or object. Just as this law loses its force, the political object must again come forward. If the whole consideration is a calculation of probability based on definite persons and relations, then the political object, being the original motive, must be an essential factor in the product. The smaller the sacrifice we demand from our opponent, the smaller, it may be expected, will be the means of resistance which he will employ; but the smaller his preparation, the smaller will ours require to be. Further, the smaller our political object, the less value shall we set upon it, and the more easily shall we be induced to give it up altogether.

Thus, therefore, the political object, as the original motive of the War, will be the standard for determining both the aim of the military force and also the amount of effort to be made. This it cannot be in itself, but it is so in relation to both the belligerent States, because we are concerned with realities, not with mere abstractions. One and the same political object may produce totally different effects upon different people, or even upon the same people at different times; we can, therefore, only admit the political object as the measure, by considering it in its effects upon those masses which it is to move, and consequently the nature of those masses also comes into consideration. It is easy to see that thus the result may be very different according as these masses are animated with a spirit which will infuse vigour into the action or otherwise. It is quite possible for such a state of feeling to exist between two States that a very trifling political motive for War may produce an effect quite disproportionate – in fact, a perfect explosion.

This applies to the efforts which the political object will call forth in the two States, and to the aim which the military action shall prescribe for itself. At times it may itself be that aim, as, for example, the conquest of a province. At other times the political object itself is not suitable for the aim of military action; then such a one must be chosen as will be an equivalent for it, and stand in its place as regards the conclusion of peace. But also, in this, due attention to the peculiar character of the States concerned is always supposed. There are circumstances in which the equivalent must be much greater than the political object, in order to secure the latter. The political object will be so much the more the standard of aim and effort, and have more influence in itself, the more the masses are indifferent, the less that any mutual feeling of hostility prevails in the two States from other causes, and therefore there are cases where the political object almost alone will be decisive.

If the aim of the military action is an equivalent for the political object, that action will in general diminish as the political object diminishes, and in a greater degree the more the political object dominates. Thus it is explained how, without any contradiction in itself, there may be Wars of all degrees of importance and energy, from a War of extermination down to the mere use of an army of observation. This, however, leads to a question of another kind which we have hereafter to develop and answer.

12. A suspension in the action of war unexplained by anything said as yet

However insignificant the political claims mutually advanced, however weak the means put forth, however small the aim to which military action is directed, can this action be suspended even for a moment? This is a question which penetrates deeply into the nature of the subject.

Every transaction requires for its accomplishment a certain time which we call its duration. This may be longer or shorter, according as the person acting throws more or less dispatch into his movements.

About this more or less we shall not trouble ourselves here. Each person acts in his own fashion; but the slow person does not protract the thing because he wishes to spend more time about it, but because by his nature he requires more time, and if he made more haste would not do the thing so well. This time, therefore, depends on subjective causes, and belongs to the length, so called, of the action.

If we allow now to every action in War this, its length, then we must assume, at first sight at least, that any expenditure of time beyond this length, that is, every suspension of hostile action, appears an absurdity; with respect to this it must not be forgotten that we now speak not of the progress of one or other of the two opponents, but of the general progress of the whole action of the War.

13. There is only one cause which can suspend the action, and this seems to be only possible on one side in any case

If two parties have armed themselves for strife, then a feeling of animosity must have moved them to it; as long now as they continue armed, that is, do not come to terms of peace, this feeling must exist; and it can only be brought to a standstill by either side by one single motive alone, which is, *that he waits for a more favourable moment for action*. Now, at first sight, it appears that this motive can never exist except on one side, because it, *eo ipso*, must be prejudicial to the other. If the one has an interest in acting, then the other must have an interest in waiting.

A complete equilibrium of forces can never produce a suspension of action, for during this suspension he who has the positive object (that is, the assailant) must continue progressing; for if we should imagine an equilibrium in this way, that he who has the positive object, therefore the strongest motive, can at the same time only command the lesser means, so that the equation is made up by the product of the motive and the power, then we must say, if no alteration in this condition of equilibrium is to be expected, the two parties must make peace; but if an alteration is to be expected, then it can only be favourable to one side, and therefore the other has a manifest interest to act without delay. We see that the conception of an equilibrium cannot explain a suspension of arms, but that it ends in the question of the *expectation of a more favourable moment*.

Let us suppose, therefore, that one of two States has a positive object, as, for instance, the conquest of one of the enemy's provinces – which is to be utilized in the settlement of peace. After this conquest, his political object is accomplished, the necessity for action ceases, and for him a pause ensues. If the adversary is also contented with this solution, he will make peace, if not, he must act. Now, if we suppose that in four weeks he will be in a better condition to act, then he has sufficient grounds for putting off the time of action.

But from that moment the logical course for the enemy appears to be to act that he may not give the conquered party *the desired* time. Of course, in this mode of reasoning a complete insight into the state of circumstances on both sides is supposed.

14. *Thus a continuance of action will ensue which will advance towards a climax*

If this unbroken continuity of hostile operations really existed, the effect would be that everything would again be driven towards the extreme; for, irrespective of the effect of such incessant activity in inflaming the feelings, and infusing into the whole a greater degree of passion, a greater elementary force, there would also follow from this continuance of action a stricter continuity, a closer connexion between cause and effect, and thus every single action would become of more importance, and consequently more replete with danger.

But we know that the course of action in War has

seldom or never this unbroken continuity, and that there have been many Wars in which action occupied by far the smallest portion of time employed, the whole of the rest being consumed in inaction. It is impossible that this should be always an anomaly; suspension of action in War must therefore be possible, that is no contradiction in itself. We now proceed to show how this is.

15. *Here, therefore, the principle of polarity is brought into requisition*

As we have supposed the interests of one Commander to be always antagonistic to those of the other, we have assumed a true *polarity*. We reserve a fuller explanation of this for another chapter, merely making the following observation on it at present.

The principle of polarity is only valid when it can be conceived in one and the same thing, where the positive and its opposite the negative completely destroy each other. In a battle both sides strive to conquer; that is true polarity, for the victory of the one side destroys that of the other. But when we speak of two different things which have a common relation external to themselves, then it is not the things but their relations which have the polarity.

16. Attack and defence are things differing in kind and of unequal force. Polarity is, therefore, not applicable to them

If there was only one form of War, to wit, the attack of the enemy, therefore no defence; or, in other words, if the attack was distinguished from the defence merely by the positive motive, which the one has and the other has not, but the methods of each were precisely one and the same: then in this sort of fight every advantage gained on the one side would be a corresponding disadvantage on the other, and true polarity would exist.

But action in War is divided into two forms, attack and defence, which, as we shall hereafter explain more particularly, are very different and of unequal strength. Polarity therefore lies in that to which both bear a relation, in the decision, but not in the attack or defence itself.

If the one Commander wishes the solution put off, the other must wish to hasten it, but only by the same form of action. If it is A's interest not to attack his enemy at present, but four weeks hence, then it is B's interest to be attacked, not four weeks hence, but at the present moment. This is the direct antagonism of interests, but it by no means follows that it would be for B's interest to attack A at once. That is plainly something totally different.

17. The effect of polarity is often destroyed by the superiority of the defence over the attack, and thus the suspension of action in war is explained

If the form of defence is stronger than that of offence, as we shall hereafter show, the question arises, Is the advantage of a deferred decision as great on the one side as the advantage of the defensive form on the other? If it is not, then it cannot by its counter-weight overbalance the latter, and thus influence the progress of the action of the War. We see, therefore, that the impulsive force existing in the polarity of interests may be lost in the difference between the strength of the offensive and the defensive, and thereby become ineffectual.

If, therefore, that side for which the present is favourable, is too weak to be able to dispense with the advantage of the defensive, he must put up with the unfavourable prospects which the future holds out; for it may still be better to fight a defensive battle in the unpromising future than to assume the offensive or make peace at present. Now, being convinced that the superiority of the defensive (rightly understood) is very great, and much greater than may appear at first sight, we conceive that the greater number of those periods of inaction which occur in war are thus explained without involving any contradiction. The weaker the motives to action are, the more will those motives be absorbed and neutralized by this difference between attack and defence, the more frequently, therefore, will action in warfare be stopped, as indeed experience teaches.

18. A second ground consists in the imperfect knowledge of circumstances

But there is still another cause which may stop action in War, viz. an incomplete view of the situation. Each Commander can only fully know his own position; that of his opponent can only be known to him by reports, which are uncertain; he may, therefore form a wrong judgement with respect to it upon data of this description, and, in consequence of that error, he may suppose that the power of taking the initiative rests with his adversary when it lies really with himself. This want of perfect insight might certainly just as often occasion an untimely action as untimely inaction, and hence it would in itself no more contribute to delay than to accelerate action in War. Still, it must always be regarded as one of the natural causes which may bring action in War to a standstill without involving a contradiction. But if we reflect how much more we are inclined and induced to estimate the power of our opponents too high than too low, because it lies in human nature to do so, we shall admit that our imperfect insight into facts in general must contribute very much to delay action in War, and to modify the application of the principles pending our conduct.

The possibility of a standstill brings into the action of War a new modification, inasmuch as it dilutes that action with the element of time, checks the influence or sense of danger in its course, and increases the means of reinstating a lost balance of force. The greater the tension of feelings from which the War springs, the greater therefore the energy with which it is carried on, so much the shorter will be the periods of inaction; on the other hand, the weaker the principle of warlike activity, the longer will be these periods: for powerful motives increase the force of the will, and this, as we know, is always a factor in the product of force.

19. Frequent periods of inaction in war remove it further from the absolute, and make it still more a calculation of probabilities

But the slower the action proceeds in War, the more frequent and longer the periods of inaction, so much the more easily can an error be repaired; therefore, so much the bolder a General will be in his calculations, so much the more readily will he keep them below the line of the absolute, and build everything upon probabilities and conjecture. Thus, according as the course of the War is more or less slow, more or less time will be allowed for that which the nature of a concrete case particularly requires, calculation of probability based on given circumstances.

20. Therefore, the element of chance only is wanting to make of war a game, and in that element it is least of all deficient

We see from the foregoing how much the objective nature of War makes it a calculation of probabilities; now there is only one single element still wanting to make it a game, and that element it certainly is not without: it is chance. There is no human affair which stands so constantly and so generally in close connexion with chance as War. But together with chance, the accidental, and along with it good luck, occupy a great place in War.

21. War is a game both objectively and subjectively

If we now take a look at the *subjective nature* of War, that is to say, at those conditions under which it is carried on, it will appear to us still more like a game. Primarily the element in which the operations of War are carried on is danger; but which of all the moral qualities is the first in danger? *Courage*. Now certainly courage is quite compatible with prudent calculation, but still they are things of quite a different kind, essentially different qualities of the mind; on the other hand, daring reliance on good fortune, boldness, rashness, are only expressions of courage, and all these propensities of the mind look for the fortuitous (or accidental), because it is their element.

We see, therefore, how, from the commencement,

the absolute, the mathematical as it is called, nowhere finds any sure basis in the calculations in the Art of War; and that from the outset there is a play of possibilities, probabilities, good and bad luck, which spreads about with all the coarse and fine threads of its web, and makes War of all branches of human activity the most like a gambling game.

22. How this accords best with the human mind in general

Although our intellect always feels itself urged towards clearness and certainty, still our mind often feels itself attracted by uncertainty. Instead of threading its way with the understanding along the narrow path of philosophical investigations and logical conclusions, in order, almost unconscious of itself, to arrive in spaces where it feels itself a stranger, and where it seems to part from all well-known objects, it prefers to remain with the imagination in the realms of chance and luck. Instead of living yonder on poor necessity, it revels here in the wealth of possibilities; animated thereby, courage then takes wings to itself, and daring and danger make the element into which it launches itself as a fearless swimmer plunges into the stream.

Shall theory leave it here, and move on, self-satisfied with absolute conclusions and rules? Then it is of no practical use. Theory must also take into account the human element; it must accord a place to courage, to boldness, even to rashness. The Art of War has to deal with living and with moral forces, the consequence of which is that it can never attain the absolute and positive. There is therefore everywhere a margin for the accidental, and just as much in the greatest things as in the smallest. As there is room for this accidental on the one hand, so on the other there must be courage and self-reliance in proportion to the room available. If these qualities are forthcoming in a high degree, the margin left may likewise be great. Courage and self-reliance are, therefore, principles quite essential to War; consequently, theory must only set up such rules as allow ample scope for all degrees and varieties of these necessary and noblest of military virtues. In daring there may still be wisdom, and prudence as well, only they are estimated by a different standard of value.

23. War is always a serious means for a serious object. Its more particular definition

Such is War; such the Commander who conducts it; such the theory which rules it. But War is no pastime; no mere passion for venturing and winning; no work of a free enthusiasm: it is a serious means for a serious object. All that appearance which it wears from the varying hues of fortune, all that it assimilates into itself of the oscillations of passion, of courage, of imagination, of enthusiasm, are only particular properties of this means.

The War of a community – of whole Nations, and particularly of civilized Nations – always starts from a political condition, and is called forth by a political motive. It is, therefore, a political act. Now if it was a perfect, unrestrained, and absolute expression of force, as we had to deduce it from its mere conception, then the moment it is called forth by policy it would step into the place of policy, and as something quite independent of it would set it aside, and only follow its own laws, just as a mine at the moment of explosion cannot be guided into any other direction than that which has been given to it by preparatory arrangements. This is how the thing has really been viewed hitherto, whenever a want of harmony between policy and the conduct of a War has led to theoretical distinctions of the kind. But it is not so, and the idea is radically false. War in the real world, as we have already seen, is not an extreme thing which expends itself at one single discharge; it is the operation of powers which do not develop themselves completely in the same manner and in the same measure, but which at one time expand sufficiently to overcome the resistance opposed by inertia or friction, while at another they are too weak to produce an effect; it is therefore, in a certain measure, a pulsation of violent force more or less vehement, consequently making its discharges and exhausting its powers more or less quickly – in other words, conducting more or less quickly to the aim, but always lasting long enough to admit of influence being exerted on it in its course, so as to give it this or that direction, in short, to be subject to the will of a guiding intelligence. Now, if we reflect that War has its root in a political object, then naturally this original motive which called it into existence should also continue the first and highest consideration in its conduct. Still, the political object is no despotic lawgiver on that account; it must accommodate itself to the nature of the means, and though changes in these means may involve modification in the political objective, the latter always retains a prior right to consideration. Policy, therefore, is interwoven with the whole action of War, and must exercise a continuous influence upon it, as far as the nature of the forces liberated by it will permit.

24. *War is a mere continuation of policy by other means*

We see, therefore, that War is not merely a political act, but also a real political instrument, a continuation of political commerce, a carrying out of the same by other means. All beyond this which is strictly peculiar to War relates merely to the peculiar nature of the means which it uses. That the tendencies and views of policy shall not be incompatible with these means, the Art of War in general and the Commander in each particular case may demand, and this claim is truly not a trifling one. But however powerfully this may react on political views in particular cases, still it must always be regarded as only a modification of them; for the political view is the object, War is the means, and the means must always include the object in our conception.

25. Diversity in the nature of wars

The greater and the more powerful the motives of a War, the more it affects the whole existence of a people. The more violent the excitement which precedes the War, by so much the nearer will the War approach to its abstract form, so much the more will it be directed to the destruction of the enemy, so much the nearer will the military and political ends coincide, so much the more purely military and less political the War appears to be; but the weaker the motives and the tensions, so much the less will the natural direction of the military element – that is, force – be coincident with the direction which the political element indicates; so much the more must, therefore, the War become diverted from its natural direction, the political object diverge from the aim of an ideal War, and the War appear to become political.

But, that the reader may not form any false conceptions, we must here observe that by this natural tendency of War we only mean the philosophical, the strictly logical, and by no means the tendency of forces actually engaged in conflict, by which would be supposed to be included all the emotions and passions of the combatants. No doubt in some cases these also might be excited to such a degree as to be with difficulty restrained and confined to the political road; but in most cases such a contradiction will not arise, because by the existence of such strenuous exertions a great plan in harmony therewith would be implied. If the plan is directed only upon a small object, then the impulses of feeling amongst the masses will be also so weak that these masses will require to be stimulated rather than repressed.

26. *They may all be regarded as political acts*

Returning now to the main subject, although it is true that in one kind of War the political element seems almost to disappear, whilst in another kind it occupies a very prominent place, we may still affirm that the one is as political as the other; for if we regard the State policy as the intelligence of the personified State, then amongst all the constellations in the political sky whose movements it has to compute, those must be included which arise when the nature of its relations imposes the necessity of a great War. It is only if we understand by policy not a true appreciation of affairs in general, but the conventional conception of a cautious, subtle, also dishonest craftiness, averse from violence, that the latter kind of War may belong more to policy than the first.

27. *Influence of this view on the right understanding of military history, and on the foundations of theory*

We see, therefore, in the first place, that under all circumstances War is to be regarded not as an independent thing, but as a political instrument; and it is only by taking this point of view that we can avoid finding ourselves in opposition to all military history. This is the only means of unlocking the great book and making it intelligible. Secondly, this view shows us how Wars must differ in character according to the nature of the motives and circumstances from which they proceed.

Now, the first, the grandest, and most decisive act of judgement which the Statesman and General exercises is rightly to understand in this respect the War in which he engages, not to take it for something, or to wish to make of it something, which by the nature of its relations it is impossible for it to be. This is, therefore, the first, the most comprehensive, of all strategical questions. We shall enter into this more fully in treating of the plan of a War.

For the present we content ourselves with having brought the subject up to this point, and having thereby fixed the chief point of view from which War and its theory are to be studied.

28. Result for theory

War is, therefore, not only chameleon-like in character, because it changes its colour in some degree in each particular case, but it is also, as a whole, in relation to the predominant tendencies which are in it, a wonderful trinity, composed of the original violence of its elements, hatred and animosity, which may be looked upon as blind instinct; of the play of probabilities and chance, which make it a free activity of the soul; and of the subordinate nature of a political instrument, by which it belongs purely to the reason.

The first of these three phases concerns more the

people; the second, more the General and his Army; the third, more the Government. The passions which break forth in War must already have a latent existence in the peoples. The range which the display of courage and talents shall get in the realm of probabilities and of chance depends on the particular characteristics of the General and his Army, but the political objects belong to the Government alone.

These three tendencies, which appear like so many different law-givers, are deeply rooted in the nature of the subject, and at the same time variable in degree. A theory which would leave any one of them out of account, or set up any arbitrary relation between them, would immediately become involved in such a contradiction with the reality, that it might be regarded as destroyed at once by that alone.

The problem is, therefore, that theory shall keep itself poised in a manner between these three tendencies, as between three points of attraction.

The way in which alone this difficult problem can be solved we shall examine in the book on the 'Theory of War'. In every case the conception of War, as here defined, will be the first ray of light which shows us the true foundation of theory, and which first separates the great masses and allows us to distinguish them from one another.

End and Means in War

Having in the foregoing chapter ascertained the complicated and variable nature of War, we shall now occupy ourselves in examining into the influence which this nature has upon the end and means in War.

If we ask, first of all, for the object upon which the whole effort of War is to be directed, in order that it may suffice for the attainment of the political object, we shall find that it is just as variable as are the political object, and the particular circumstances of the War.

If, in the next place, we keep once more to the pure conception of War, then we must say that the political object properly lies out of its province, for if War is an act of violence to compel the enemy to fulfil our will, then in every case all depends on our overthrowing the enemy, that is, disarming him, and on that alone. This object, developed from abstract conceptions, but which is also the one aimed at in a great many cases in reality, we shall, in the first place, examine in this reality.

In connexion with the plan of a campaign we shall hereafter examine more closely into the meaning of disarming a nation, but here we must at once draw a distinction between three things, which, as three general objects, comprise everything else within them. They are the *military power*, *the country*, and *the will of the enemy*.

The *military power* must be destroyed, that is, reduced

to such a state as not to be able to prosecute the War. This is the sense in which we wish to be understood hereafter, whenever we use the expression 'destruction of the enemy's military power'.

The *country* must be conquered, for out of the country a new military force may be formed.

But even when both these things are done, still the War, that is, the hostile feeling and action of hostile agencies, cannot be considered as at an end as long as the *will* of the enemy is not subdued also; that is, its Government and its Allies must be forced into signing a peace, or the people into submission; for whilst we are in full occupation of the country, the War may break out afresh, either in the interior or through assistance given by Allies. No doubt, this may also take place after a peace, but that shows nothing more than that every War does not carry in itself the elements for a complete decision and final settlement.

But even if this is the case, still with the conclusion of peace a number of sparks are always extinguished which would have smouldered on quietly, and the excitement of the passions abates, because all those whose minds are disposed to peace, of which in all nations and under all circumstances there is always a great number, turn themselves away completely from the road to resistance. Whatever may take place subsequently, we must always look upon the object as attained, and the business of War as ended, by a peace.

Branches of the Art of War

War in its literal meaning is fighting, for fighting alone is the efficient principle in the manifold activity which in a wide sense is called War. But fighting is a trial of strength of the moral and physical forces by means of the latter. That the moral cannot be omitted is evident of itself, for the condition of the mind has always the most decisive influence on the forces employed in War.

The necessity of fighting very soon led men to special inventions to turn the advantage in it in their own favour: in consequence of these the mode of fighting has undergone great alterations; but in whatever way it is conducted its conception remains unaltered, and fighting is that which constitutes War.

The inventions have been from the first weapons and equipments for the individual combatants. These have to be provided and the use of them learnt before the War begins. They are made suitable to the nature of the fighting, consequently are ruled by it; but plainly the activity engaged in these appliances is a different thing from the fight itself; it is only the preparation for the combat, not the conduct of the same. That arming and equipping are not essential to the conception of fighting is plain, because mere wrestling is also fighting.

Fighting has determined everything appertaining to arms and equipment, and these in turn modify the mode

On the Nature of War

of fighting; there is, therefore, a reciprocity of action between the two.

Nevertheless, the fight itself remains still an entirely special activity, more particularly because it moves in an entirely special element, namely, in the element of danger.

If, then, there is anywhere a necessity for drawing a line between two different activities, it is here; and in order to see clearly the importance of this idea, we need only just to call to mind how often eminent personal fitness in one field has turned out nothing but the most useless pedantry in the other.

It is also in no way difficult to separate in idea the one activity from the other, if we look at the combatant forces fully armed and equipped as a given means, the profitable use of which requires nothing more than a knowledge of their general results.

The Art of War is therefore, in its proper sense, the art of making use of the given means in fighting, and we cannot give it a better name than the *'Conduct of War'*. On the other hand, in a wider sense all activities which have their existence on account of War, therefore the whole creation of troops, that is levying them, arming, equipping, and exercising them, belong to the Art of War.

To make a sound theory it is most essential to separate these two activities, for it is easy to see that if every act of War is to begin with the preparation of military forces, and to presuppose forces so organized as a primary condition for conducting War, that theory will only be applicable in the few cases to which the force available happens to be exactly suited. If, on the other hand, we wish to have a theory which shall suit most cases, and will not be wholly useless in any case, it must be founded on those means which are in most general use, and in respect to these only on the actual results springing from them.

The conduct of War is, therefore, the formation and conduct of the fighting. If this fighting was a single act, there would be no necessity for any further subdivision, but the fight is composed of a greater or less number of single acts, complete in themselves, which we call combats, as we have shown in the first chapter of the first book, and which form new units. From this arises the totally different activities, that of the *formation* and *conduct* of these single combats in themselves, and the *combination* of them with one another, with a view to the ultimate object of the War. The first is called *tactics*, the other *strategy*.

This division into tactics and strategy is now in almost general use, and every one knows tolerably well under which head to place any single fact, without knowing very distinctly the grounds on which the classification is founded. But when such divisions are blindly adhered to in practice, they must have some deep root. We have searched for this root, and we might say that it is just the usage of the majority which has brought us to it. On the other hand, we look upon the arbitrary, unnatural definitions of these conceptions sought to be established by some writers as not in accordance with the general usage of the terms.

According to our classification, therefore, tactics *is the theory of the use of military forces in combat.* Strategy *is the theory of the use of combats for the object of the War.*

The way in which the conception of a single, or independent combat, is more closely determined, the conditions to which this unit is attached, we shall only be able to explain clearly when we consider the combat; we must content ourselves for the present with saying that in relation to space, therefore in combats taking place at the same time, the unit reaches just as far as *personal command* reaches; but in regard to time, and therefore in relation to combats which follow each other in close succession, it reaches to the moment when the crisis which takes place in every combat is entirely passed.

That doubtful cases may occur, cases, for instance, in which several combats may perhaps be regarded also as a single one, will not overthrow the ground of distinction we have adopted, for the same is the case with all grounds of distinction of real things which are differentiated by a gradually diminishing scale. There may, therefore, certainly be acts of activity in War which, without any alteration in the point of view, may just as well be counted strategic as tactical; for example, very extended positions resembling a chain of posts, the preparations for the passage of a river at several points, etc.

Our classification reaches and covers only the *use of the military force*. But now there are in War a number of activities which are subservient to it, and still are quite different from it; sometimes closely allied, sometimes less near in their affinity. All these activities relate to the *maintenance of the military force*. In the same way as its creation and training precede its use, so its maintenance is always a necessary condition. But, strictly viewed, all activities thus connected with it are always to be regarded only as preparations for fighting; they are certainly nothing more than activities which are very close to the action, so that they run through the hostile act alternate in importance with the use of the forces. We have therefore a right to exclude them as well as the other preparatory activities from the Art of War in its restricted sense, from the conduct of War properly so called; and we are obliged to do so if we would comply with the first principle of all theory, the elimination of all heterogeneous elements. Who would include in the real 'conduct of War' the whole litany of subsistence and administration, because it is admitted to stand in constant reciprocal action with the use of the troops, but is something essentially different from it?

We have said, in the third chapter of our first book, that as the fight or combat is the only directly effective activity, therefore the threads of all others, as they end in it, are included in it. By this we meant to say that to all others an object was thereby appointed which, in accordance with the laws peculiar to themselves, they must seek to attain. Here we must go a little closer into this subject.

The subjects which constitute the activities outside of the combat are of various kinds.

The one part belongs, in one respect, to the combat itself, is identical with it, whilst it serves in another respect for the maintenance of the military force. The other part belongs purely to the subsistence, and has only, in consequence of the reciprocal action, a limited influence on the combats by its results. The subjects which in one respect belong to the fighting itself are *marches*, *camps*, and *cantonments*, for they suppose so many different situations of troops, and where troops are supposed there the idea of the combat must always be present.

The other subjects, which only belong to the maintenance, are *subsistence*, *care of the sick*, the *supply and repair of arms and equipment*.

Marches are quite identical with the use of the troops. The act of marching in the *combat*, generally called manoeuvring, certainly does not necessarily include the use of weapons, but it is so completely and necessarily combined with it that it forms an integral part of that which we call a combat. But the march outside the combat is nothing but the execution of a strategic measure. By the strategic plan is settled *when, where, and with what forces* a battle is to be delivered – and to carry that into execution the march is the only means.

The march outside of the combat is therefore an instrument of strategy, but not on that account exclusively a subject of strategy, for as the armed force which executes it may be involved in a possible combat at any moment, therefore its execution stands also under tactical as well as strategic rules. If we prescribe to a column its route on a particular side of a river or of a branch of a mountain, then that is a strategic measure, for it contains the intention of fighting on that particular side of the hill or river in preference to the other, in case a combat should be necessary during the march.

But if a column, instead of following the road through a valley, marches along the parallel ridge of heights, or for the convenience of marching divides itself into several columns, then these are tactical arrangements, for they relate to the manner in which we shall use the troops in the anticipated combat.

The particular order of march is in constant relation with readiness for combat, is therefore tactical in its nature, for it is nothing more than the first or preliminary disposition for the battle which may possibly take place.

As the march is the instrument by which strategy apportions its active elements, the combats, but these last often only appear by their results and not in the details of their real course, it could not fail to happen that in theory the instrument has often been substituted for the efficient principle. Thus we hear of a decisive skilful march, allusion being thereby made to those combat-combinations to which these marches led. This substitution of ideas is too natural and conciseness of expression too desirable to call for alteration, but still it is only a condensed chain of ideas in regard to which we must never omit to bear in mind the full meaning, if we would avoid falling into error.

We fall into an error of this description if we attribute to strategical combinations a power independent of tactical results. We read of marches and manoeuvres combined, the object attained, and at the same time not a word about combat, from which the conclusion is drawn that there are means in War of conquering an enemy without fighting. The prolific nature of this error we cannot show until hereafter.

But although a march can be regarded absolutely as an integral part of the combat, still there are in it certain relations which do not belong to the combat, and therefore are neither tactical nor strategic. To these belong all arrangements which concern only the accommodation of the troops, the construction of bridges, roads, etc. These are only conditions; under many circumstances they are in very close connexion, and may almost identify themselves with the troops, as in building a bridge in presence of the enemy; but in themselves they are always extraneous activities, the theory of which does not form part of the theory of the conduct of War.

Camps, by which we mean every disposition of troops in concentrated, therefore in battle order, in contradistinction to cantonments or quarters, are a state of rest, therefore of restoration; but they are at the same time also the strategic appointment of a battle on the spot chosen; and by the manner in which they are taken up they contain the fundamental lines of the battle, a condition from which every defensive battle starts; they are therefore essential parts of both strategy and tactics.

Cantonments take the place of camps for the better refreshment of the troops. They are therefore, like camps, strategic subjects as regards position and extent; tactical subjects as regards internal organization, with a view to readiness to fight.

The occupation of camps and cantonments no doubt usually combines with the recuperation of the troops another object also, for example, the covering a district of country, the holding a position; but it can very well be only the first. We remind our readers that strategy may follow a great diversity of objects, for everything which appears an advantage may be the object of a combat, and the preservation of the instrument with which War is made must necessarily very often become the object of its partial combinations.

If, therefore, in such a case strategy ministers only to the maintenance of the troops, we are not on that account out of the field of strategy, for we are still engaged with the use of the military force, because every disposition of that force upon any point whatever of the theatre of War is such a use.

But if the maintenance of the troops in camp or quarters calls forth activities which are no employment of the armed force, such as the construction of huts, pitching of tents, subsistence and sanitary services in camps or quarters, then such belong neither to strategy nor tactics.

Even entrenchments, the site and preparation of which are plainly part of the order of battle, therefore tactical subjects, do not belong to the theory of the conduct of War so far as respects the *execution of their construction*, the knowledge and skill required for such work being, in point of fact, qualities inherent in the nature of an organized Army; the theory of the combat takes them for granted.

Amongst the subjects which belong to the mere keeping up of an armed force, because none of the parts are identified with the combat, the victualling of the troops themselves comes first, as it must be done almost daily and for each individual. Thus it is that it completely permeates military action in the parts constituting strategy – we say parts constituting strategy, because during a battle the subsistence of troops will rarely have any influence in modifying the plan, although the thing is conceivable enough. The care for the subsistence of the troops comes therefore into reciprocal action chiefly with strategy, and there is nothing more common than for the leading strategic features of a campaign and War to be traced out in connexion with a view to this supply. But however frequent and however important these views of supply may be, the subsistence of the troops always remains a completely different activity from the use of the troops, and the former has only an influence on the latter by its results.

The other branches of administrative activity which we have mentioned stand much further apart from the use of the troops. The care of sick and wounded, highly important as it is for the good of an Army, directly affects it only in a small portion of the individuals composing it, and therefore has only a weak and indirect influence upon the use of the rest. The completing and replacing articles of arms and equipment, except so far as by the organism of the forces it constitutes a continuous activity inherent in them – takes place only periodically, and therefore seldom affects strategic plans.

We must, however, here guard ourselves against a mistake. In certain cases these subjects may be really of decisive importance. The distance of hospitals and depots of munitions may very easily be imagined as the sole cause of very important strategic decisions. We do not wish either to contest that point or to throw it into the shade. But we are at present occupied not with the particular facts of a concrete case, but with abstract theory; and our assertion therefore is that such an influence is too rare to give the theory of sanitary measures and the supply of munitions and arms an importance in the theory of the conduct of War such as to make it worth while to include in the theory of the conduct of War the consideration of the different ways and systems which the above theories may furnish, in the same way as is certainly necessary in regard to victualling troops.

If we have clearly understood the results of our reflections, then the activities belonging to War divide themselves into two principal classes, into such as are only *'preparations for War'* and into the *'War itself'*. This division must therefore also be made in theory.

The knowledge and applications of skill in the preparations for War are engaged in the creation, discipline, and maintenance of all the military forces; what general names should be given to them we do not enter into, but we see that artillery, fortification, elementary tactics, as they are called, the whole organization and administration of the various armed forces, and all such things are included. But the theory of War itself occupies itself with the use of these prepared means for the object of the war. It needs of the first only the results, that is, the knowledge of the principal properties of the means taken in hand for use. This we call 'The Art of War' in a limited sense, or 'Theory of the Conduct of War', or 'Theory of the Employment of Armed Forces', all of them denoting for us the same thing.

The present theory will therefore treat the combat as the real contest, marches, camps, and cantonments as circumstances which are more or less identical with it. The subsistence of the troops will only come into consideration like *other given instances* in respect of its results, not as an activity belonging to the combat.

The Art of War thus viewed in its limited sense divides itself again into tactics and strategy. The former occupies itself with the form of the separate combat, the latter with its use. Both connect themselves with the circumstances of marches, camps, cantonments only through the combat, and these circumstances are tactical or strategic according as they relate to the form or to the signification of the battle.

No doubt there will be many readers who will consider superfluous this careful separation of two things lying so close together as tactics and strategy, because it has no direct effect on the conduct itself of War. We admit, certainly that it would be pedantry to look for direct effects on the field of battle from a theoretical distinction.

But the first business of every theory is to clear up conceptions and ideas which have been jumbled together, and, we may say, entangled and confused; and only when a right understanding is established, as to names and conceptions, can we hope to progress with clearness and facility, and be certain that author and reader will always see things from the same point of view. Tactics and strategy are two activities mutually permeating each other in time and space, at the same time essentially different activities, the inner laws and mutual relations of which cannot be intelligible at all to the mind until a clear conception of the nature of each activity is established.

He to whom all this is nothing, must either repudiate all theoretical consideration, *or his understanding has not as yet been pained* by the confused and perplexing ideas resting on no fixed point of view, leading to no satisfactory result, sometimes dull, sometimes fantastic, sometimes floating in vague generalities, which we are often obliged to hear and read on the conduct of War, owing to the spirit of scientific investigation having hitherto been little directed to these subjects.

On the Theory of War

1. The first conception of the 'Art of War' was merely the preparation of the armed forces

Formerly by the term 'Art of War', or 'Science of War', nothing was understood but the totality of those branches of knowledge and those appliances of skill occupied with material things. The pattern and preparation and the mode of using arms, the construction of fortifications and entrenchments, the organism of an army and the mechanism of its movements, were the subject of these branches of knowledge and skill above referred to, and the end and aim of them all was the establishment of an armed force fit for use in War. All this concerned merely things belonging to the material world and a one-sided activity only, and it was in fact nothing but an activity advancing by gradations from the lower occupations to a finer kind of mechanical art. The relation of all this to War itself was very much the same as the relation of the art of the sword cutler to the art of using the sword. The employment in the moment of danger and in a state of constant reciprocal action of the particular energies of mind and spirit in the direction proposed to them was not yet even mooted.

2. True war first appears in the art of sieges

In the art of sieges we first perceive a certain degree of guidance of the combat, something of the action of the intellectual faculties upon the material forces placed under their control, but generally only so far that it very soon embodied itself again in new material forms, such as approaches, trenches, counter-approaches, batteries, etc., and every step which this action of the higher faculties took was marked by some such result; it was only the thread that was required on which to string these material inventions in order. As the intellect can hardly manifest itself in this kind of War, except in such things, so therefore nearly all that was necessary was done in that way.

3. Then tactics tried to find its way in the same direction

Afterwards tactics attempted to give to the mechanism of its joints the character of a general disposition, built upon the peculiar properties of the instrument, which character leads indeed to the battlefield, but instead of leading to the free activity of mind, leads to an Army made like an automaton by its rigid formations and orders of battle, which, movable only by the word of command, is intended to unwind its activities like a piece of clockwork.

4. The real conduct of war only made its appearance incidentally and incognito

The conduct of War properly so called, that is, a use of the prepared means adapted to the most special requirements, was not considered as any suitable subject for theory, but one which should be left to natural talents alone. By degrees, as War passed from the hand-to-hand encounters of the middle ages into a more regular and systematic form, stray reflections on this point also forced themselves into men's minds, but they mostly appeared only incidentally in memoirs and narratives, and in a certain measure incognito.

5. Reflections on military events brought about the want of a theory

As contemplation on War continually increased, and its history every day assumed more of a critical character, the urgent want appeared of the support of fixed maxims and rules, in order that in the controversies naturally arising about military events the war of opinions might be brought to some one point. This whirl of opinions, which neither revolved on any central pivot nor according to any appreciable laws, could not but be very distasteful to people's minds.

6. Endeavours to establish a positive theory

There arose, therefore, an endeavour to establish maxims, rules, and even systems for the conduct of War. By this the attainment of a positive object was proposed, without taking into view the endless difficulties which the conduct of War presents in that respect. The conduct of War, as we have shown, has no definite limits in any direction, while every system has the circumscribing nature of a synthesis, from which results an irreconcileable opposition between such a theory and practice.

7. Limitation to material objects

Writers on theory felt the difficulty of the subject soon enough, and thought themselves entitled to get rid of it by directing their maxims and systems only upon material things and a one-sided activity. Their aim was to reach results, as in the science for the preparation for War, entirely certain and positive, and therefore only to take into consideration that which could be made matter of calculation.

8. Superiority of numbers

The superiority in numbers being a material condition, it was chosen from amongst all the factors required to produce victory, because it could be brought under mathematical laws through combinations of time and space. It was thought possible to leave out of sight all other circumstances, by supposing them to be equal on each side, and therefore to neutralize one another. This would have been very well if it had been done to gain a preliminary knowledge of this one factor, according to its relations, but to make it a rule for ever to consider superiority of numbers as the sole law; to see the whole secret of the Art of War in the formula, *in a certain time, at a certain point, to bring up superior masses* – was a restriction overruled by the force of realities.

9. *Victualling of troops*

By one theoretical school an attempt was made to systematize another material element also, by making the subsistence of troops, according to a previously established organism of the Army, the supreme legislator in the higher conduct of War. In this way certainly they arrived at definite figures, but at figures which rested on a number of arbitrary calculations, and which therefore could not stand the test of practical application.

10. *Base*

An ingenious author tried to concentrate in a single conception, that of a *Base*, a whole host of objects, amongst which sundry relations even with immaterial forces found their way in as well. The list comprised the subsistence of the troops, the keeping them complete in numbers and equipment, the security of communications with the home country, lastly, the security of retreat in case it became necessary; and, first of all, he proposed to substitute this conception of a base for all these things; then for the base itself to substitute its own length (extent); and, last of all, to substitute the angle formed by the army with this base: all this was done merely to obtain a pure geometrical result utterly useless. This last is, in fact, unavoidable, if we reflect that none of these substitutions could be made without violating truth and leaving out some of the things contained in the original conception. The idea of a base is a real necessity for strategy, and to have conceived it is meritorious; but to make such a use of it as we have depicted is completely inadmissible, and could not but lead to partial conclusions which have forced these theorists into a direction opposed to common sense, namely, to a belief in the decisive effect of the enveloping form of attack.

11. Interior Lines

As a reaction against this false direction, another geometrical principle, that of the so-called interior lines, was then elevated to the throne. Although this principle rests on a sound foundation, on the truth that the combat is the only effectual means in War, still it is, just on account of its purely geometrical nature, nothing but another case of one-sided theory which can never gain ascendancy in the real world.

12. All these attempts are open to objection

All these attempts at theory are only to be considered in their analytical part as progress in the province of truth, but in their synthetical part, in their precepts and rules, they are quite unserviceable.

They strive after determinate quantities, whilst in War all is undetermined, and the calculation has always to be made with varying quantities.

They direct the attention only upon material forces, while the whole military action is penetrated throughout by intelligent forces and their effects.

They only pay regard to activity on one side, whilst War is a constant state of reciprocal action, the effects of which are mutual.

13. As a rule they exclude genius

All that was not attainable by such miserable philosophy, the offspring of partial views, lay outside the precincts of science – and was the field of genius, which *raises itself above rules*.

Pity the warrior who is contented to crawl about in this beggardom of rules, which are too bad for genius, over which it can set itself superior, over which it can perchance make merry! What genius does must be the best of all rules, and theory cannot do better than to show how and why it is so.

Pity the theory which sets itself in opposition to the

mind! It cannot repair this contradiction by any humility, and the humbler it is so much the sooner will ridicule and contempt drive it out of real life.

14. The difficulty of theory as soon as moral quantities come into consideration

Every theory becomes infinitely more difficult from the moment that it touches on the province of moral quantities. Architecture and painting know quite well what they are about as long as they have only to do with matter; there is no dispute about mechanical or optical construction. But as soon as the moral activities begin their work, as soon as moral impressions and feelings are produced, the whole set of rules dissolves into vague ideas.

The science of medicine is chiefly engaged with bodily phenomena only; its business is with the animal organism, which, liable to perpetual change, is never exactly the same for two moments. This makes its practice very difficult, and places the judgement of the physician above his science; but how much more difficult is the case if a moral effect is added, and how much higher must we place the physician of the mind?

15. The moral quantities must not be excluded in war

But now the activity in War is never directed solely against matter; it is always at the same time directed against the intelligent force which gives life to this matter, and to separate the two from each other is impossible.

But the intelligent forces are only visible to the inner eye, and this is different in each person, and often different in the same person at different times.

As danger is the general element in which everything moves in War, it is also chiefly by courage, the feeling of one's own power, that the judgement is differently influenced. It is to a certain extent the crystalline lens through which all appearances pass before reaching the understanding.

And yet we cannot doubt that these things acquire a certain objective value simply through experience.

Every one knows the moral effect of a surprise, of an attack in flank or rear. Every one thinks less of the enemy's courage as soon as he turns his back, and ventures much more in pursuit than when pursued. Every one judges of the enemy's General by his reputed talents, by his age and experience, and shapes his course accordingly. Every one casts a scrutinizing glance at the spirit and feeling of his own and the enemy's troops. All these and similar effects in the province of the moral nature of man have established themselves by experience, are perpetually recurring, and therefore warrant our reckoning them as real quantities of their kind. What could we do with any theory which should leave them out of consideration?

Certainly experience is an indispensable title for these truths. With psychological and philosophical sophistries no theory, no General, should meddle.

16. Principal difficulty of a theory for the conduct of war

In order to comprehend clearly the difficulty of the proposition which is contained in a theory for the conduct of War, and thence to deduce the necessary characteristics of such a theory, we must take a closer view of the chief particulars which make up the nature of activity in War.

17. First speciality – moral forces and their effects (Hostile feeling)

The first of these specialities consists in the moral forces and effects.

The combat is, in its origin, the expression of *hostile feeling*, but in our great combats, which we call Wars, the hostile feeling frequently resolves itself into merely a hostile *view*, and there is usually no innate hostile feeling residing in individual against individual. Nevertheless, the combat never passes off without such feelings being brought into activity. National hatred, which is seldom wanting in our Wars, is a substitute for personal hostility in the breast of individual opposed to individual. But where this also is wanting, and at first no animosity of feeling subsists, a hostile feeling is kindled by the combat itself; for an act of violence which any one commits upon us by order of his superior, will excite in us a desire to retaliate and be revenged on him, sooner than on the superior power at whose command the act was done. This is human, or animal if we will; still it is so. We are very apt to regard the combat in theory as an abstract trial of strength, without any participation on the part of the feelings, and that is one of the thousand errors which theorists deliberately commit, because they do not see its consequences.

Besides that excitation of feelings naturally arising from the combat itself, there are others also which do not essentially belong to it, but which, on account of their relationship, easily unite with it – ambition, love of power, enthusiasm of every kind, etc., etc.

18. *The impressions of danger (Courage)*

Finally, the combat begets the element of danger, in which all the activities of War must live and move, like the bird in the air or the fish in the water. But the influences of danger all pass into the feelings, either directly – that is, instinctively – or through the medium of the understanding. The effect in the first case would be a desire to escape from the danger, and, if that cannot be done, fright and anxiety. If this effect does not take place, then it is *courage*, which is a counterpoise to that instinct. Courage is, however, by no means an act of the understanding, but likewise a feeling, like fear; the latter looks to the physical preservation, courage to the moral preservation. Courage, then, is a nobler instinct. But because it is so, it will not allow itself to be used as a lifeless instrument, which produces its effects exactly according to prescribed measure. Courage is therefore no mere counterpoise to danger in order to neutralize the latter in its effects, but a peculiar power in itself.

19. *Extent of the influence of danger*

But to estimate exactly the influence of danger upon the principal actors in War, we must not limit its sphere to the physical danger of the moment. It dominates over the actor, not only by threatening him, but also by threatening all entrusted to him, not only at the moment in which it is actually present, but also through the imagination at all other moments, which have a connexion with the present; lastly, not only directly by itself, but also indirectly by the responsibility which makes it bear with tenfold weight on the mind of the chief actor. Who could advise, or resolve upon a great battle, without feeling his mind more or less wrought up, or perplexed by, the danger and responsibility which such a great act of decision carries in itself? We may say that action in War, in so far as it is real action, not a mere condition, is never out of the sphere of danger.

20. *Other powers of feeling*

If we look upon these affections which are excited by hostility and danger as peculiarly belonging to War, we do not, therefore, exclude from it all others accompanying man in his life's journey. They will also find room here frequently enough. Certainly we may say that many a petty action of the passions is silenced in this serious business of life; but that holds good only in respect to those acting in a lower sphere, who, hurried on from one state of danger and exertion to another, lose sight of the rest of the things of life, *become unused to deceit*, because it is of no avail with death, and so attain to that soldierly simplicity of character which has always been the best representative of the military profession. In higher regions it is otherwise, for the higher a man's rank, the more he must look around him; then arise interests on every side, and a manifold activity of the passions of good and bad. Envy and generosity, pride and humility, fierceness and tenderness, all may appear as active powers in this great drama.

21. Peculiarity of mind

The peculiar characteristics of mind in the chief actor have, as well as those of the feelings, a high importance. From an imaginative, flighty, inexperienced head, and from a calm, sagacious understanding, different things are to be expected.

22. From the diversity in mental individualities arises the diversity of ways leading to the end

It is this great diversity in mental individuality, the influence of which is to be supposed as chiefly felt in the higher ranks, because it increases as we progress upwards, which chiefly produces the diversity of ways leading to the end noticed by us in the first book, and which gives, to the play of probabilities and chance, such an unequal share in determining the course of events.

23. Second peculiarity – living reaction

The second peculiarity in War is the living reaction, and the reciprocal action resulting therefrom. We do not here speak of the difficulty of estimating that reaction, for that is included in the difficulty before mentioned, of treating the moral powers as quantities; but of this, that reciprocal action, by its nature, opposes anything like a regular plan. The effect which any measure produces upon the enemy is the most distinct of all the data which action affords; but every theory must keep to classes (or groups) of phenomena, and can never take up the really individual case in itself: that must everywhere be left to judgement and talent. It is therefore natural that in a business such as War, which in its plan – built upon general circumstances – is so often thwarted by unexpected and singular accidents, more must generally be left to talent; and less use can be made of a *theoretical guide* than in any other.

24. Third peculiarity – uncertainty of all data

Lastly, the great uncertainty of all data in War is a peculiar difficulty, because all action must, to a certain extent, be planned in a mere twilight, which in addition not unfrequently – like the effect of a fog or moonshine – gives to things exaggerated dimensions and an unnatural appearance.

What this feeble light leaves indistinct to the sight talent must discover, or must be left to chance. It is therefore again talent, or the favour of fortune, on which reliance must be placed, for want of objective knowledge.

25. Positive theory is impossible

With materials of this kind we can only say to ourselves that it is a sheer impossibility to construct for the Art of War a theory which, like a scaffolding, shall ensure to the chief actor an external support on all sides. In all those cases in which he is thrown upon his talent he would find himself away from this scaffolding of theory and in opposition to it, and, however many-sided it might be framed, the same result would ensue of which we spoke when we said that talent and genius act beyond the law, and theory is in opposition to reality.

26. Means left by which a theory is possible (The difficulties are not everywhere equally great)

Two means present themselves of getting out of this difficulty. In the first place, what we have said of the nature of military action in general does not apply in the same manner to the action of every one, whatever may be his standing. In the lower ranks the spirit of self-sacrifice is called more into request, but the difficulties which the understanding and judgement meet with are infinitely less. The field of occurrences is more confined. Ends and means are fewer in number. Data more distinct; mostly also contained in the actually visible. But the higher we ascend the more the difficulties increase, until in the Commander-in-Chief they reach their climax, so that with him almost everything must be left to genius.

Further, according to a division of the subject in *agreement with its nature*, the difficulties are not everywhere the same, but diminish the more results manifest themselves in the material world, and increase the more they pass into the moral, and become motives which influence the will. Therefore it is easier to determine, by theoretical rules, the order and conduct of a battle, than the use to be made of the battle itself. Yonder physical weapons clash with each other, and although mind is not wanting therein, matter must have its rights. But in the effects to be produced by battles when the material results become motives, we have only to do with the moral nature. In a word, it is easier to make a theory for *tactics* than for *strategy*.

27. Theory must be of the nature of observation, not of doctrine

The second opening for the possibility of a theory lies in the point of view that it does not necessarily require to be a *direction* for action. As a general rule, whenever an *activity* is for the most part occupied with the same objects over and over again, with the same ends and means, although there may be trifling alterations and a corresponding number of varieties of combination, such things are capable of becoming a subject of study for the reasoning faculties. But such study is just the most essential part of every *theory*, and has a peculiar title to that name. It is an analytical investigation of the subject that leads to an exact knowledge; and if brought to bear on the results of experience, which in our case would be military history, to a thorough familiarity with it. The nearer theory attains the latter object, so much the more it passes over from the objective form of knowledge into the subjective one of skill in action; and so much the more, therefore, it will prove itself effective when circumstances allow of no other decision but that of personal talents; it will show its effects in that talent itself. If theory investigates the subjects which constitute War; if it separates more distinctly that which at first sight seems amalgamated; if it explains fully the properties of the means; if it shows their probable effects; if it makes evident the nature of objects; if it brings to bear all over the field of War the light of essentially critical investigation – then it has fulfilled the chief duties of its province. It becomes then a guide to him who wishes to make himself acquainted with War from books; it lights up the whole road for him, facilitates his progress, educates his judgement, and shields him from error.

If a man of expertness spends half his life in the endeavour to clear up an obscure subject thoroughly, he will probably know more about it than a person who seeks to master it in a short time. Theory is instituted that each person in succession may not have to go through the same labour of clearing the ground and toiling through his subject, but may find the thing in order, and light admitted on it. It should educate the mind of the future leader in War, or rather guide him in his self-instruction, but not accompany him to the field of battle; just as a sensible tutor forms and enlightens the opening mind of a youth without, therefore, keeping him in leading strings all through his life.

If maxims and rules result of themselves from the considerations which theory institutes, if the truth accretes itself into that form of crystal, then theory will not oppose this natural law of the mind; it will rather, if the arch ends in such a keystone, bring it prominently out; but so does this, only in order to satisfy the philosophical law of reason, in order to show distinctly the point to which the lines all converge, not in order to form out of it an algebraical formula for use upon the battlefield; for even these maxims and rules serve more to determine in the reflecting mind the leading outline of its habitual movements than as landmarks indicating to it the way in the act of execution.

28. By this point of view theory becomes possible, and ceases to be in contradiction to practice

Taking this point of view, there is a possibility afforded of a satisfactory, that is, of a useful, theory of the conduct of War, never coming into opposition with the reality, and it will only depend on rational treatment to bring it so far into harmony with action that between theory and practice there shall no longer be that absurd difference which an unreasonable theory, in defiance of common sense, has often produced, but which, just as often, narrow-mindedness and ignorance have used as a pretext for giving way to their natural incapacity.

29. Theory therefore considers the nature of ends and means – ends and means in tactics

Theory has therefore to consider the nature of the means and ends.

In tactics the means are the disciplined armed forces which are to carry on the contest. The object is victory. The precise definition of this conception can be better explained hereafter in the consideration of the combat. Here we content ourselves by denoting the retirement of the enemy from the field of battle as the sign of victory. By means of this victory strategy gains the object for which it appointed the combat, and which constitutes its special signification. This signification has certainly some influence on the nature of the victory. A victory which is intended to weaken the enemy's armed forces is a different thing from one which is designed only to put us in possession of a position. The signification of a combat may therefore have a sensible influence on the preparation and conduct of it, consequently will be also a subject of consideration in tactics.

30. Circumstances which always attend the application of the means

As there are certain circumstances which attend the combat throughout, and have more or less influence upon its result, therefore these must be taken into consideration in the application of the armed forces.

These circumstances are the locality of the combat (ground), the time of day, and the weather.

31. Locality

The locality, which we prefer leaving for solution, under the head of 'Country and Ground', might, strictly speaking, be without any influence at all if the combat took place on a completely level and uncultivated plain.

In a country of steppes such a case may occur, but in the cultivated countries of Europe it is almost an imaginary idea. Therefore a combat between civilized nations, in which country and ground have no influence, is hardly conceivable.

32. Time of day

The time of day influences the combat by the difference between day and night; but the influence naturally extends further than merely to the limits of these divisions, as every combat has a certain duration, and great battles last for several hours. In the preparations for a great battle, it makes an essential difference whether it begins in the morning or the evening. At the same time, certainly many battles may be fought in which the question of the time of day is quite immaterial, and in the generality of cases its influence is only trifling.

33. Weather

Still more rarely has the weather any decisive influence, and it is mostly only by fogs that it plays a part.

34. End and means in strategy

Strategy has in the first instance only the victory, that is, the tactical result, as a means to its object, and ultimately those things which lead directly to peace. The application of its means to this object is at the same time attended by circumstances which have an influence thereon more or less.

35. Circumstances which attend the application of the means of strategy

These circumstances are country and ground, the former including the territory and inhabitants of the whole theatre of war; next the time of the day, and the time of the year as well; lastly, the weather, particularly any unusual state of the same, severe frost, etc.

36. These form new means

By bringing these things into combination with the results of a combat, strategy gives this result – and therefore the combat – a special signification, places before it a particular object. But when this object is not that which leads directly to peace, therefore a subordinate one, it is only to be looked upon as a means; and therefore in strategy we may look upon the results of combats or victories, in all their different significations, as means. The conquest of a position is such a result of a combat applied to ground. But not only are the different combats with special objects to be considered as means, but also every higher aim which we may have in view in the combination of battles directed on a common object is to be regarded as a means. A winter campaign is a combination of this kind applied to the season.

There remain, therefore, as objects, only those things which may be supposed as leading *directly* to peace.

On the Nature of War

Theory investigates all these ends and means according to the nature of their effects and their mutual relations.

37. Strategy deduces only from experience the ends and means to be examined

The first question is, How does strategy arrive at a complete list of these things? If there is to be a philosophical inquiry leading to an absolute result, it would become entangled in all those difficulties which the logical necessity of the conduct of War and its theory exclude. It therefore turns to experience, and directs its attention on those combinations which military history can furnish. In this manner, no doubt, nothing more than a limited theory can be obtained, which only suits circumstances such as are presented in history. But this incompleteness is unavoidable, because in any case theory must either have deduced from, or have compared with, history what it advances with respect to things. Besides, this incompleteness in every case is more theoretical than real.

One great advantage of this method is that theory cannot lose itself in abstruse disquisitions, subtleties, and chimeras, but must always remain practical.

38. How far the analysis of the means should be carried

Another question is, How far should theory go in its analysis of the means? Evidently only so far as the elements in a separate form present themselves for consideration in practice. The range and effect of different weapons is very important to tactics; their construction, although these effects result from it, is a matter of indifference; for the conduct of War is not making powder and cannon out of a given quantity of charcoal, sulphur, and saltpetre, of copper and tin: the given quantities for the conduct of War are arms in a finished state and their effects. Strategy makes use of maps without troubling itself about triangulations; it does not inquire how the country is subdivided into departments and provinces, and how the people are educated and governed, in order to attain the best military results; but it takes things as it finds them in the community of European States, and observes where very different conditions have a notable influence on War.

39. Great simplification of the knowledge required

That in this manner the number of subjects for theory is much simplified, and the knowledge requisite for the conduct of War much reduced, is easy to perceive. The very great mass of knowledge and appliances of skill which minister to the action of War in general, and which are necessary before an army fully equipped can take the field, unite in a few great results before they are able to reach, in actual War, the final goal of their activity; just as the streams of a country unite themselves in rivers before they fall into the sea. Only those activities emptying themselves directly into the sea of War have to be studied by him who is to conduct its operations.

40. *This explains the rapid growth of great generals, and why a general is not a man of learning*

This result of our considerations is in fact so necessary, that any other would have made us distrustful of their accuracy. Only thus is explained how so often men have made their appearance with great success in War, and indeed in the higher ranks even in supreme Command, whose pursuits had been previously of a totally different nature; indeed how, as a rule, the most distinguished Generals have never risen from the very learned or really erudite class of officers, but have been mostly men who, from the circumstances of their position, could not have attained to any great amount of knowledge. On that account those who have considered it necessary or even beneficial to commence the education of a future General by instruction in all details have always been ridiculed as absurd pedants. It would be easy to show the injurious tendency of such a course, because the human mind is trained by the knowledge imparted to it and the direction given to its ideas. Only what is great can make it great; the little can only make it little, if the mind itself does not reject it as something repugnant.

41. Former contradictions

Because this simplicity of knowledge requisite in War was not attended to, but that knowledge was always jumbled up with the whole impedimenta of subordinate sciences and arts, therefore the palpable opposition to the events of real life which resulted could not be solved otherwise than by ascribing it all to genius, which requires no theory and for which no theory could be prescribed.

42. On this account all use of knowledge was denied, and everything ascribed to natural talents

People with whom common sense had the upper hand felt sensible of the immense distance remaining to be filled up between a genius of the highest order and a learned pedant; and they became in a manner free-thinkers, rejected all belief in theory, and affirmed the conduct of War to be a natural function of man, which he performs more or less well according as he has brought with him into the world more or less talent in that direction. It cannot be denied that these were nearer to the truth than those who placed a value on false knowledge; at the same time it may easily be seen that such a view is itself but an exaggeration. No activity of the human understanding is possible without a certain stock of ideas; but these are, for the greater part at least, not innate but acquired, and constitute his knowledge. The only question therefore is, of what kind should these ideas be; and we think we have answered it if we say that they should be directed on those things which man has directly to deal with in War.

43. The knowledge must be made suitable to the position

Inside this field of military activity, the knowledge required must be different according to the station of the Commander. It will be directed on smaller and more circumscribed objects if he holds an inferior, upon greater and more comprehensive ones if he holds a higher situation. There are Field Marshals who would not have shone at the head of a cavalry regiment, and vice versa.

44. The knowledge in war is very simple, but not, at the same time, very easy

But although the knowledge in War is simple, that is to say directed to so few subjects, and taking up those only in their final results, the art of execution is not, on that account, easy. Of the difficulties to which activity in War is subject generally, we have already spoken in the first book; we here omit those things which can only be overcome by courage, and maintain also that the activity of mind is only simple and easy in inferior stations, but increases in difficulty with increase of rank, and in the highest position, in that of Commander-in-Chief, is to be reckoned amongst the most difficult which there is for the human mind.

45. *Of the nature of this knowledge*

The Commander of an Army neither requires to be a learned explorer of history nor a publicist, but he must be well versed in the higher affairs of State; he must know and be able to judge correctly of traditional tendencies, interests at stake, the immediate questions at issue, and the characters of leading persons; he need not be a close observer of men, a sharp dissector of human character, but he must know the character, the feelings, the habits, the peculiar faults and inclinations of those whom he is to command. He need not understand anything about the make of a carriage, or the harness of a battery horse, but he must know how to calculate exactly the march of a column, under different circumstances, according to the time it requires. These are matters the knowledge of which cannot be forced out by an apparatus of scientific formula and machinery: they are only to be gained by the exercise of an accurate judgement in the observation of things and of men, aided by a special talent for the apprehension of both.

The necessary knowledge for a high position in military action is therefore distinguished by this, that by observation, therefore by study and reflection, it is only to be attained through a special talent which as an intellectual instinct understands how to extract from the phenomena of life only the essence or spirit, as bees do the honey from the flowers; and that it is also to be gained by experience of life as well as by study and reflection. Life will never bring forth a Newton or an Euler by its rich teachings, but it may bring forth great calculators in War, such as Condé or Frederick.

It is therefore not necessary that, in order to vindicate the intellectual dignity of military activity, we should resort to untruth and silly pedantry. There never has been a great and distinguished Commander of contracted mind, but very numerous are the instances of men who, after serving with the greatest distinction in inferior positions, remained below mediocrity in the highest, from insufficiency of intellectual capacity. That even amongst those holding the post of Commander-in-Chief there may be a difference according to the degree of their plenitude of power is a matter of course.

46. Science must become art

Now we have yet to consider one condition which is more necessary for the knowledge of the conduct of War than for any other, which is, that it must pass completely into the mind and almost completely cease to be something objective. In almost all other arts and occupations of life the active agent can make use of truths which he has only learnt once, and in the spirit and sense of which he no longer lives, and which he extracts from dusty books. Even truths which he has in hand and uses daily may continue something external to himself. If the architect takes up a pen to settle the strength of a pier by a complicated calculation, the truth found as a result is no emanation from his own mind. He had first to find the data with labour, and then to submit these to an operation of the mind, the rule for which he did not discover, the necessity of which he is perhaps at the moment only partly conscious of, but which he applies, for the most part, as if by mechanical dexterity. But it is never so in War. The moral reaction, the ever-changeful form of things, makes it necessary for the chief actor to carry in himself the whole mental apparatus of his knowledge, that anywhere and at every pulse-beat he may be capable of giving the requisite decision from himself. Knowledge must, by this complete assimilation with his own mind and life, be converted into real power. This is the reason why everything seems so easy with men distinguished in War, and why everything is ascribed to natural talent. We say natural talent, in order thereby to distinguish it from that which is formed and matured by observation and study.

We think that by these reflections we have explained the problem of a theory of the conduct of War, and pointed out the way to its solution.

Of the two fields into which we have divided the conduct of War, tactics and strategy, the theory of the latter contains unquestionably, as before observed, the greatest difficulties, because the first is almost limited to a circumscribed field of objects, but the latter, in the direction of objects leading directly to peace, opens to itself an unlimited field of possibilities. Since for the most part the Commander-in-Chief has only to keep these objects steadily in view, therefore the part of strategy in which he moves is also that which is particularly subject to this difficulty.

Theory, therefore, especially where it comprehends the highest services, will stop much sooner in strategy than in tactics at the simple consideration of things, and content itself to assist the Commander to that insight into things which, blended with his whole thought, makes his course easier and surer, never forces him into opposition with himself in order to obey an objective truth.

Art or Science of War

1. Usage still unsettled (Power and knowledge. Science when mere knowing; Art, when doing, is the object)

The choice between these terms seems to be still unsettled, and no one seems to know rightly on what grounds it should be decided, and yet the thing is simple. We have already said elsewhere that 'knowing' is something different from 'doing'. The two are so different that they should not easily be mistaken the one for the other. The 'doing' cannot properly stand in any book, and therefore also Art should never be the title of a book. But because we have once accustomed ourselves to combine in conception, under the name of theory of Art, or simply Art, the branches of knowledge (which may be separately pure sciences) necessary for the practice of an Art, therefore it is consistent to continue this ground of distinction, and to call everything Art when the object is to carry out the 'doing' (being able), as for example, Art of building; Science, when merely knowledge is the object; as Science of mathematics, of astronomy. That in every Art certain complete sciences may be included is intelligible of itself, and should not perplex us. But still it is worth observing that there is also no science without a mixture of Art. In mathematics, for instance, the use of figures and of algebra is an Art, but that is only one amongst many instances. The reason is, that however plain and palpable the difference is between knowledge and power in the composite results of human knowledge, yet it is difficult to trace out their line of separation in man himself.

2. Difficulty of separating perception from judgement (Art of war)

All thinking is indeed Art. Where the logician draws the line, where the premises stop which are the result of cognition – where judgement begins, there Art begins. But more than this: even the perception of the mind is judgement again, and consequently Art; and at last, even the perception by the senses as well. In a word, if it is impossible to imagine a human being possessing merely the faculty of cognition, devoid of judgement or the reverse, so also Art and Science can never be completely separated from each other. The more these subtle elements of light embody themselves in the outward forms of the world, so much the more separate appear their domains; and now once more, where the object is creation and production, there is the province of Art; where the object is investigation and knowledge Science holds sway. After all this it results of itself that it is more fitting to say Art of War than Science of War.

So much for this, because we cannot do without these conceptions. But now we come forward with the assertion that War is neither an Art nor a Science in the real signification, and that it is just the setting out from that starting-point of ideas which has led to a wrong direction being taken, which has caused War to be put on a par with other arts and sciences, and has led to a number of erroneous analogies.

This has indeed been felt before now, and on that account it was maintained that War is a handicraft; but there was more lost than gained by that, for a handicraft is only an inferior art, and as such is also subject to definite and rigid laws. In reality the Art of War did go on for some time in the spirit of a handicraft – we allude to the times of the Condottieri – but then it received that direction, not from intrinsic but from external causes; and military history shows how little it was at that time in accordance with the nature of the thing.

3. War is part of the intercourse of the human race

We say therefore War belongs not to the province of Arts and Sciences, but to the province of social life. It is a conflict of great interests which is settled by bloodshed, and only in that is it different from others. It would be better, instead of comparing it with any Art, to liken it to business competition, which is also a conflict of human interests and activities; and it is still more like State policy, which again, on its part, may be looked upon as a kind of business competition on a great scale. Besides, State policy is the womb in which War is developed, in which its outlines lie hidden in a rudimentary state, like the qualities of living creatures in their germs.

4. Difference

The essential difference consists in this, that War is no activity of the will, which exerts itself upon inanimate matter like the mechanical Arts; or upon a living but still passive and yielding subject, like the human mind and the human feelings in the ideal Arts, but against a living and reacting force. How little the categories of Arts and Sciences are applicable to such an activity strikes us at once; and we can understand at the same time how that constant seeking and striving after laws like those which may be developed out of the dead material world could not but lead to constant errors. And yet it is just the mechanical Arts that some people would imitate in the Art of War. The imitation of the ideal Arts was quite out of the question, because these themselves dispense too much with laws and rules, and those hitherto tried, always acknowledged as insufficient and one-sided, are perpetually undermined and washed away by the current of opinions, feelings, and customs.

Whether such a conflict of the living, as takes place and is settled in War, is subject to general laws, and whether these are capable of indicating a useful line of action, will be partly investigated in this book; but so much is evident in itself, that this, like every other subject which does not surpass our powers of understanding, may be lighted up, and be made more or less plain in its inner relations by an inquiring mind, and that alone is sufficient to realize the idea of a *theory*.

Methodicism

In order to explain ourselves clearly as to the conception of method, and method of action, which play such an important part in War, we must be allowed to cast a hasty glance at the logical hierarchy through which, as through regularly constituted official functionaries, the world of action is governed.

Law, in the widest sense strictly applying to perception as well as action, has plainly something subjective and arbitrary in its literal meaning, and expresses just that on which we and those things external to us are dependent. As a subject of cognition, *Law* is the relation of things and their effects to one another; as a subject of the will, it is a motive of action, and is then equivalent to *command* or *prohibition*.

Principle is likewise such a law for action, except that it has not the formal definite meaning, but is only the spirit and sense of law in order to leave the judgement more freedom of application when the diversity of the real world cannot be laid hold of under the definite form of a law. As the judgement must of itself suggest the cases in which the principle is not applicable, the latter therefore becomes in that way a real aid or guiding star for the person acting.

Principle is *objective* when it is the result of objective truth, and consequently of equal value for all men; it is *subjective*, and then generally called *Maxim* if there are subjective relations in it, and if it therefore has a certain value only for the person himself who makes it.

Rule is frequently taken in the sense of *Law*, and then means the same as *Principle*, for we say 'no rule without exceptions', but we do not say 'no law without exceptions', a sign that with *Rule* we retain to ourselves more freedom of application.

In another meaning *Rule* is the means used of discerning a recondite truth in a particular sign lying close at hand, in order to attach to this particular sign the law of action directed upon the whole truth. Of this kind are all the rules of games of play, all abridged processes in mathematics, etc.

Directions and *instructions* are determinations of action which have an influence upon a number of minor circumstances too numerous and unimportant for general laws.

Lastly, *Method, mode of acting*, is an always recurring proceeding selected out of several possible ones; and *Methodicism* (METHODISMUS) is that which is determined by method instead of by general principles or particular prescriptions. By this the cases which are placed under such methods must necessarily be supposed alike in their essential parts. As they cannot all be this, then the point is that at least as many as possible should be; in other words, that Method should be calculated on the most probable cases. Methodicism is therefore not founded on determined particular premises, but on the average probability of cases one with another; and its ultimate tendency is to set up an average truth, the constant and uniform application of which soon acquires something of the nature of a mechanical appliance, which in the end does that which is right almost unwittingly.

The conception of law in relation to perception is not necessary for the conduct of War, because the complex phenomena of War are not so regular, and the regular are not so complex, that we should gain anything more by this conception than by the simple truth. And where a simple conception and language is sufficient, to resort to the complex becomes affected and pedantic. The conception of law in relation to action cannot be used in the theory of the conduct of War, because owing to the variableness and diversity of the phenomena there is in it no determination of such a general nature as to deserve the name of law.

But principles, rules, prescriptions, and methods are conceptions indispensable to a theory of the conduct of War, in so far as that theory leads to positive doctrines, because in doctrines the truth can only crystallize itself in such forms.

As tactics is the branch of the conduct of War in which theory can attain the nearest to positive doctrine, therefore these conceptions will appear in it most frequently.

Not to use cavalry against unbroken infantry except in some case of special emergency, only to use firearms within effective range in the combat, to spare the forces as much as possible for the final struggle – these are tactical principles. None of them can be applied absolutely in every case, but they must always be present to the mind of the Chief, in order that the benefit of the truth contained in them may not be lost in cases where that truth can be of advantage.

If from the unusual cooking by an enemy's camp his movement is inferred, if the intentional exposure of troops in a combat indicates a false attack, then this way of discerning the truth is called rule, because from a single visible circumstance that conclusion is drawn which corresponds with the same.

If it is a rule to attack the enemy with renewed vigour, as soon as he begins to limber up his artillery in the combat, then on this particular fact depends a course of action which is aimed at the general situation of the enemy as inferred from the above fact, namely, that he is about to give up the fight, that he is commencing to draw off his troops, and is neither capable of making a serious stand while thus drawing off nor of making his retreat gradually in good order.

Regulations and *methods* bring preparatory theories into the conduct of War, in so far as disciplined troops are inoculated with them as active principles. The whole body of instructions for formations, drill, and field service are regulations and methods: in the drill instructions the first predominate, in the field service instructions the latter. To these things the real conduct of War attaches itself; it takes them over, therefore, as given modes of proceeding, and as such they must appear in the theory of the conduct of War.

But for those activities retaining freedom in the employment of these forces there cannot be regulations, that is, definite instructions, because they would do away with freedom of action. Methods, on the other hand, as a general way of executing duties as they arise, calculated as we have said, on an average of probability, or as a dominating influence of principles and rules carried through to application, may certainly appear in the theory of the conduct of War, provided only they are not represented as something different from what they are, not as the absolute and necessary modes of action (systems), but as the best of general forms which may be used as shorter ways in place of a particular disposition for the occasion, at discretion.

But the frequent application of methods will be seen to be most essential and unavoidable in the conduct of War, if we reflect how much action proceeds on mere conjecture, or in complete uncertainty, because one side is prevented from learning all the circumstances which influence the dispositions of the other, or because, even if these circumstances which influence the decisions of the one were really known, there is not, owing to their extent and the dispositions they would entail, sufficient time for the other to carry out all necessary counteracting measures – that therefore measures in War must always be calculated on a certain number of possibilities; if we reflect how numberless are the trifling things belonging to any single event, and which therefore should be taken into account along with it, and that therefore there is no other means to suppose the one counteracted by the other, and to base our arrangements only upon what is of a general nature and probable; if we reflect lastly that, owing to the increasing number of officers as we descend the scale of rank, less must be left to the true discernment and ripe judgement of individuals the lower the sphere of action, and that when we reach those ranks where we can look for no other notions but those which the regulations of the service and experience afford, we must help them with the methodic forms bordering on those regulations. This will serve both as a support to their judgement and a barrier against those extravagant and erroneous views which are so especially to be dreaded in a sphere where experience is so costly.

Besides this absolute need of method in action, we must also acknowledge that it has a positive advantage, which is that, through the constant repetition of a formal exercise, a readiness, precision, and firmness is attained in the movement of troops which diminishes the natural friction, and makes the machine move easier.

Method will therefore be the more generally used, become the more indispensable, the further down the scale of rank the position of the active agent; and on the other hand, its use will diminish upwards, until in the highest position it quite disappears. For this reason it is more in its place in tactics than in strategy.

War in its highest aspects consists not of an infinite number of little events, the diversities in which compensate each other, and which therefore by a better or worse method are better or worse governed, but of separate great decisive events which must be dealt with separately. It is not like a field of stalks, which, without any regard to the particular form of each stalk, will be mowed better or worse, according as the mowing instrument is good or bad, but rather as a group of large trees, to which the axe must be laid with judgement, according to the particular form and inclination of each separate trunk.

How high up in military activity the admissibility of method in action reaches naturally determines itself, not according to actual rank, but according to things; and it affects the highest positions in a less degree, only because these positions have the most comprehensive subjects of activity. A constant order of battle, a constant formation of advance guards and outposts, are methods by which a General ties not only his subordinates' hands, but also his own in certain cases. Certainly they may have been devised by himself, and may be applied by him according to circumstances, but they may also be a subject of theory, in so far as they are based on the general properties of troops and weapons. On the other hand, any method by which definite plans for wars or campaigns are to be given out all ready made as if from a machine are absolutely worthless.

As long as there exists no theory which can be sustained, that is, no enlightened treatise on the conduct of War, method in action cannot but encroach beyond its proper limits in high places, for men employed in these spheres of activity have not always had the opportunity of educating themselves, through study and through contact with the higher interests. In the impracticable and inconsistent disquisitions of theorists and critics they cannot find their way, their sound common sense rejects them, and as they bring with them no knowledge but that derived from experience, therefore in those cases which admit of, and require, a free individual treatment they readily make use of the means which experience gives them – that is, an imitation of the particular methods practised by great Generals, by which a method of action then arises of itself. If we see Frederick the Great's Generals always making their appearance in the so-called oblique order of battle, the Generals of the French Revolution always using turning movements with a long extended line of battle, and Buonaparte's lieutenants rushing to the attack with the bloody energy of concentrated masses, then we recognize in the recurrence of the mode of proceeding evidently an adopted method, and see therefore that method of action can reach up to regions bordering on the highest. Should an improved theory facilitate the study of the conduct of War, form the mind and judgement of men who are rising to the highest commands, then also method in action will no longer reach so far, and so much of it as is to be considered indispensable will then at least be formed from theory itself, and not take place out of mere imitation. However pre-eminently a great Commander does things, there is always something subjective in the way he does them; and if he has a certain manner, a large share of his individuality is contained in it which does not always accord with the individuality of the person who copies his manner.

At the same time, it would neither be possible nor right to banish subjective methodicism or manner completely from the conduct of War: it is rather to be regarded as a manifestation of that influence which the general character of a War has upon its separate events, and to which satisfaction can only be done in that way if theory is not able to foresee this general character and include it in its considerations. What is more natural than that the War of the French Revolution had its own way of doing things? and what theory could ever have included that peculiar method? The evil is only that such a manner originating in a special case easily outlives itself, because it continues whilst circumstances imperceptibly change. This is what theory should prevent by lucid and rational criticism. When in the year 1806 the Prussian Generals, Prince Louis at Saalfeld, Tauentzien on the Dornberg near Jena, Grawert before and Rüchel behind Kappellendorf, all threw themselves into the open jaws of destruction in the oblique order of Frederick the Great and managed to ruin Hohenlohe's Army in a way that no Army was ever ruined, even on the field of battle, all this was done through a manner which had outlived its day, together with the most downright stupidity to which methodicism ever led.

Criticism

The influence of theoretical principles upon real life is produced more through criticism than through doctrine, for as criticism is an application of abstract truth to real events, therefore it not only brings truth of this description nearer to life, but also accustoms the understanding more to such truths by the constant repetition of their application. We therefore think it necessary to fix the point of view for criticism next to that for theory.

From the simple narration of an historical occurrence which places events in chronological order, or at most only touches on their more immediate causes, we separate the *critical*.

In this *critical* three different operations of the mind may be observed.

First, the historical investigation and determining of doubtful facts. This is properly historical research, and has nothing in common with theory.

Secondly, the tracing of effects to causes. This is the *real critical inquiry*; it is indispensable to theory, for everything which in theory is to be established, supported, or even merely explained, by experience can only be settled in this way.

Thirdly, the testing of the means employed. This is *criticism, properly speaking*, in which praise and censure is contained. This is where theory helps history, or rather, the teaching to be derived from it.

In these two last strictly critical parts of historical study, all depends on tracing things to their primary elements, that is to say, up to undoubted truths, and not, as is so often done, resting half-way, that is, on some arbitrary assumption or supposition.

As respects the tracing of effect to cause, that is often attended with the insuperable difficulty that the real causes are not known. In none of the relations of life does this so frequently happen as in War, where events are seldom fully known, and still less motives, as the latter have been, perhaps purposely, concealed by the chief actor, or have been of such a transient and accidental character that they have been lost for history. For this reason critical narration must generally proceed hand in hand with historical investigation, and still such a want of connexion between cause and effect will often present itself, that it does not seem justifiable to consider effects as the necessary results of known causes. Here, therefore, voids must occur, that is, historical results which cannot be made use of for teaching. All that theory can demand is that the investigation should be rigidly conducted up to that point, and there leave off without drawing conclusions. A real evil springs up only if the known is made perforce to suffice as an explanation of effects, and thus a false importance is ascribed to it.

Besides this difficulty, critical inquiry also meets with another great and intrinsic one, which is that the progress of events in War seldom proceeds from one simple cause, but from several in common, and that it therefore is not sufficient to follow up a series of events to their origin in a candid and impartial spirit, but that it is then also necessary to apportion to each contributing cause its due weight. This leads, therefore, to a closer investigation of their nature, and thus a critical investigation may lead into what is the proper field of theory.

The critical *consideration*, that is, the testing of the means, leads to the question, Which are the effects peculiar to the means applied, and whether these effects were comprehended in the plans of the person directing?

The effects peculiar to the means lead to the investigation of their nature, and thus again into the field of theory.

We have already seen that in criticism all depends upon attaining to positive truth; therefore, that we must not stop at arbitrary propositions which are not allowed by others, and to because he has not found one to please him, or because he has not yet been able to make himself master of one, will at least occasionally make use of a piece of one, as one would use a ruler, to show the blunders committed by a General. The most of them are incapable of reasoning without using as a help here and there some shreds of scientific military theory. The smallest of these fragments, consisting in mere scientific words and metaphors, are often nothing more than ornamental flourishes of critical narration. Now it is in the nature of things that all technical and scientific expressions which belong to a system lose their propriety, if they ever had any, as soon as they are distorted, and used as general axioms, or as small crystalline talismans, which have more power of demonstration than simple speech.

Thus it has come to pass that our theoretical and critical books, instead of being straightforward, intelligible dissertations, in which the author always knows at least what he says and the reader what he reads, are brimful of these technical terms, which form dark points of interference where author and reader part company. But frequently they are something worse, being nothing but hollow shells without any kernel. The author himself has no clear perception of what he means, contents himself with vague ideas, which if expressed in plain language would be unsatisfactory even to himself.

A third fault in criticism is the *misuse* of *historical examples*, and a display of great reading or learning. What the history of the Art of War is we have already said, and we shall further explain our views on examples and on military history in general in special chapters. One fact merely touched upon in a very cursory manner may be used to support the most opposite views, and three or four such facts of the most heterogeneous description, brought together out of the most distant lands and remote times and heaped up, generally distract and bewilder the judgement and understanding without demonstrating anything; for when exposed to the light they turn out to be only trumpery rubbish, made use of to show off the author's learning.

But what can be gained for practical life by such obscure, partly false, confused arbitrary conceptions? So little is gained that theory on account of them has always been a true antithesis of practice, and frequently a subject of ridicule to those whose soldierly qualities in the field are above question.

But it is impossible that this could have been the case, if theory in simple language, and by natural treatment of those things which constitute the Art of making War, had merely sought to establish just so much as admits of being established; if, avoiding all false pretensions and irrelevant display of scientific forms and historical parallels, it had kept close to the subject, and gone hand in hand with those who must conduct affairs in the field by their own natural genius.

On Examples

Examples from history make everything clear, and furnish the best description of proof in the empirical sciences. This applies with more force to the Art of War than to any other. General Scharnhorst, whose handbook is the best ever written on actual War, pronounces historical examples to be of the first importance, and makes an admirable use of them himself. Had he survived the War in which he fell, the fourth part of his revised treatise on artillery would have given a still greater proof of the observing and enlightened spirit in which he sifted matters of experience.

But such use of historical examples is rarely made by theoretical writers; the way in which they more commonly make use of them is rather calculated to leave the mind unsatisfied, as well as to offend the understanding. We therefore think it important to bring specially into view the use and abuse of historical examples.

Unquestionably the branches of knowledge which lie at the foundation of the Art of War come under the denomination of empirical sciences; for although they are derived in a great measure from the nature of things, still we can only learn this very nature itself for the most part from experience; and besides that, the practical application is modified by so many circumstances that the effects can never be completely learnt from the mere nature of the means.

The effects of gunpowder, that great agent in our military activity, were only learnt by experience, and up to this hour experiments are continually in progress in order to investigate them more fully. That an iron ball to which powder has given a velocity of 1,000 feet in a second, smashes every living thing which it touches in its course is intelligible in itself; experience is not required to tell us that; but in producing this effect how many hundred circumstances are concerned, some of which can only be learnt by experience! And the physical is not the only effect which we have to study, it is the moral which we are in search of, and that can only be ascertained by experience; and there is no other way of learning and appreciating it but by experience. In the middle ages, when firearms were first invented, their effect, owing to their rude make, was materially but trifling compared to what it now is, but their effect morally was much greater. One must have witnessed the firmness of one of those masses taught and led by Buonaparte, under the heaviest and most unintermittent cannonade, in order to understand what troops, hardened by long practice in the field of danger, can do, when by a career of victory they have reached the noble principle of demanding from themselves their utmost efforts. In pure conception no one would believe it. On the other hand, it is well known that there are troops in the service of European Powers at the present moment who would easily be dispersed by a few cannon shots.

But no empirical science, consequently also no theory

of the Art of War, can always corroborate its truths by historical proof; it would also be, in some measure, difficult to support experience by single facts. If any means is once found efficacious in War, it is repeated; one nation copies another, the thing becomes the fashion, and in this manner it comes into use, supported by experience, and takes its place in theory, which contents itself with appealing to experience in general in order to show its origin, but not as a verification of its truth.

But it is quite otherwise if experience is to be used in order to overthrow some means in use, to confirm what is doubtful, or introduce something new; then particular examples from history must be quoted as proofs.

Now, if we consider closely the use of historical proofs, four points of view readily present themselves for the purpose.

First, they may be used merely as an *explanation* of an idea. In every abstract consideration it is very easy to be misunderstood, or not to be intelligible at all: when an author is afraid of this, an exemplification from history serves to throw the light which is wanted on his idea, and to ensure his being intelligible to his reader.

Secondly, it may serve as an *application* of an idea, because by means of an example there is an opportunity of showing the action of those minor circumstances which cannot all be comprehended and explained in any general expression of an idea; for in that consists, indeed, the difference between theory and experience. Both these cases belong to examples properly speaking, the two following belong to historical proofs.

Thirdly, a historical fact may be referred to particularly, in order to support what one has advanced. This is in all cases sufficient, if we have *only* to prove the *possibility* of a fact or effect.

Lastly, in the fourth place, from the circumstantial detail of a historical event, and by collecting together several of them, we may deduce some theory, which therefore has its true *proof* in this testimony itself.

For the first of these purposes all that is generally required is a cursory notice of the case, as it is only used partially. Historical correctness is a secondary consideration; a case invented might also serve the purpose as well, only historical ones are always to be preferred, because they bring the idea which they illustrate nearer to practical life.

The second use supposes a more circumstantial relation of events, but historical authenticity is again of secondary importance, and in respect to this point the same is to be said as in the first case.

For the third purpose the mere quotation of an undoubted fact is generally sufficient. If it is asserted that fortified positions may fulfil their object under certain conditions, it is only necessary to mention the position of Bunzelwitz in support of the assertion.

But if, through the narrative of a case in history, an abstract truth is to be demonstrated, then everything in the case bearing on the demonstration must be analysed in the most searching and complete manner; it must, to a certain extent, develop itself carefully before the eyes of the reader. The less effectually this is done the weaker will be the proof, and the more necessary it will be to supply the demonstrative proof which is wanting in the single case by a number of cases, because we have a right to suppose that the more minute details which we are unable to give neutralize each other in the effects in a certain number of cases.

If we want to show by example derived from experience that cavalry are better placed behind than in a line with infantry; that it is very hazardous without a decided preponderance of numbers to attempt an enveloping movement, with widely separated columns, either on a field of battle or in the theatre of war – that is, either tactically or strategically – then in the first of these cases it would not be sufficient to specify some lost battles in which the cavalry was on the flanks and some gained in which the cavalry was in rear of the infantry; and in the latter of these cases it is not sufficient to refer to the battles of Rivoli and Wagram, to the attack of the Austrians on the theatre of war in Italy, in 1796, or of the French upon the German theatre of war in the same year. The way in which these orders of battle or plans of attack essentially contributed to disastrous issues in those particular cases must be shown by closely tracing out circumstances and occurrences. Then it will appear how far such forms or measures are to be condemned, a point which it is very necessary to show, for a total condemnation would be inconsistent with truth.

It has been already said that when a circumstantial detail of facts is impossible, the demonstrative power which is deficient may to a certain extent be supplied by the number of cases quoted; but this is a very dangerous method of getting out of the difficulty, and one which has been much abused. Instead of one well-explained example, three or four are just touched upon, and thus a show is made of strong evidence. But there are matters where a whole dozen of cases brought forward would prove nothing, if, for instance, they are facts of frequent occurrence, and therefore a dozen other cases with an opposite result might just as easily be brought forward. If any one will instance a dozen lost battles in which the side beaten attacked in separate converging columns, we can instance a dozen that have been gained in which the same order was adopted. It is evident that in this way no result is to be obtained.

Upon carefully considering these different points, it will be seen how easily examples may be misapplied.

An occurrence which, instead of being carefully analysed in all its parts, is superficially noticed, is like an object seen at a great distance, presenting the same appearance on each side, and in which the details of its parts cannot be distinguished. Such examples have, in reality, served to support the most contradictory opinions. To some Daun's campaigns are models of prudence and skill. To others, they are nothing but examples of timidity and want of resolution. Buonaparte's passage across the Noric Alps in 1797 may be made to appear the noblest resolution, but also as an act of sheer temerity. His strategic defeat in 1812 may be represented as the consequence either of an excess, or of a deficiency, of energy. All these opinions have been broached, and it is easy to see that they might very well arise, because each person takes a different view of the connexion of events. At the same time these antagonistic opinions cannot be reconciled with each other, and therefore one of the two must be wrong.

Much as we are obliged to the worthy Feuquières for the numerous examples introduced in his memoirs – partly because a number of historical incidents have thus been preserved which might otherwise have been lost, and partly because he was one of the first to bring theoretical, that is, abstract, ideas into connexion with the practical in war, in so far that the cases brought forward may be regarded as intended to exemplify and confirm what is theoretically asserted – yet, in the opinion of an impartial reader, he will hardly be allowed to have attained the object he proposed to himself, that of proving theoretical principles by historical examples. For although he sometimes relates occurrences with great minuteness, still he falls short very often of showing that the deductions drawn necessarily proceed from the inner relations of these events.

Another evil which comes from the superficial notice of historical events, is that some readers are either wholly ignorant of the events, or cannot call them to remembrance sufficiently to be able to grasp the author's meaning, so that there is no alternative between either accepting blindly what is said, or remaining unconvinced.

It is extremely difficult to put together or unfold historical events before the eyes of a reader in such a way as is necessary, in order to be able to use them as proofs; for the writer very often wants the means, and can neither afford the time nor the requisite space; but we maintain that, when the object is to establish a new or doubtful opinion, one single example, thoroughly analysed, is far more instructive than ten which are superficially treated. The great mischief of these superficial representations is not that the writer puts his story forward as a proof when it has only a false title, but that he has not made himself properly acquainted with the subject, and that from this sort of slovenly, shallow treatment of history, a hundred false views and attempts at the construction of theories arise, which would never have made their appearance if the writer had looked upon it as his duty to deduce from the strict connexion of events everything new which he brought to market, and sought to prove from history.

When we are convinced of these difficulties in the use of historical examples, and at the same time of the necessity (of making use of such examples), then we shall also come to the conclusion that the latest military history is naturally the best field from which to draw them, inasmuch as it alone is sufficiently authentic and detailed.

In ancient times, circumstances connected with War, as well as the method of carrying it on, were different; therefore its events are of less use to us either theoretically or practically; in addition to which, military history, like every other, naturally loses in the course of time a number of small traits and lineaments originally to be seen, loses in colour and life, like a worn-out or darkened picture; so that perhaps at last only the large masses and leading features remain, which thus acquire undue proportions.

If we look at the present state of warfare, we should say that the Wars since that of the Austrian succession are almost the only ones which, at least as far as armament, have still a considerable similarity to the present, and which, notwithstanding the many important changes which have taken place both great and small, are still capable of affording much instruction. It is quite otherwise with the War of the Spanish succession, as the use of firearms had not then so far advanced towards perfection, and cavalry still continued the most important arm. The further we go back, the less useful becomes military history, as it gets so much the more meagre and barren of detail. The most useless of all is that of the old world.

But this usefulness is not altogether absolute, it relates only to those subjects which depend on a knowledge of minute details, or on those things in which the method of conducting war has changed. Although we know very little about the tactics in the battles between the Swiss and the Austrians, the Burgundians and French, still we find in them unmistakable evidence that they were the first in which the superiority of a good infantry over the best cavalry was displayed. A general glance at the time of the Condottieri teaches us how the whole method of conducting War is dependent on the instrument used; for at no period have the forces used in War had so much the characteristics of a special instrument, and been a class so totally distinct from the rest of the national community. The memorable way in which the Romans in the second Punic War attacked the Carthaginian possessions in Spain and Africa, while Hannibal still maintained himself in Italy, is a most instructive subject to study, as the general relations of the States and Armies concerned in the indirect act of defence are sufficiently well known.

But the more things descend into particulars and deviate in character from the most general relations, the less we can look for examples and lessons of experience from very remote periods for we have neither the means of judging properly of corresponding events, nor can we apply them to our completely different method of War.

Unfortunately, however, it has always been the fashion with historical writers to talk about ancient times. We shall not say how far vanity and charlatanism may have had a share in this, but in general we fail to discover any honest intention and earnest endeavour to instruct and convince, and we can therefore only look upon such quotations and references as embellishments to fill up gaps and hide defects.

It would be an immense service to teach the Art of War entirely by historical examples, as Feuquières proposed to do; but it would be full work for the whole life of a man, if we reflect that he who undertakes it must first qualify himself for the task by a long personal experience in actual War.

Whoever, stirred by ambition, undertakes such a task, let him prepare himself for his pious undertaking as for a long pilgrimage; let him give up his time, spare no sacrifice, fear no temporal rank or power, and rise above all feelings of personal vanity, of false shame, in order, according to the French code, to speak *the Truth, the whole Truth, and nothing but the Truth*.